WOLFGANG BORSICH

TRAVEL GUIDE
LANZAROTE

EDITORIAL YAIZA S.L.

CONTENTS

FOREWORD

Dear reader,

It gives me great pleasure to present this travel guide to you. A lot of travel books and guides are written at a distance, or the authors have too little time to really get to know the places they are describing. This book is different.

Our author, Wolfgang Borsich, has lived on Lanzarote for over 15 years, during which time he has got to know every corner of the island. Lanzarote has become his second home, and he has written numerous articles and books on it. Then there is his excellent knowledge of the language. Spanish is now his second mother tongue. So as a native of Lanzarote, I can truthfully claim that this book has been researched and written by an expert who feels deep ties with our island and its people.

This is really two books in one. Part I and Part II describe the Canary Isles, Lanzarote, and the inhabitants, in detail, for anyone who wants more in-depth information. Part III is the service section, designed as a reference work to help you discover the island yourself, with recommended restaurants and accommodation, and essential information, all up to the minute.

I hope you enjoy using this unusual travel guide.

With best wishes from your Editor,
Nieves González Hernández

FIRST IMPRESSIONS

L anzarote is no ordinary island. Formed by volcanic eruptions, this isle is unique and original. The very earth is turned inside out, more than a third of the island is covered by black lava and grey tuff, clinker and volcanic sand. Streams of lava, hardened over the years, but still seemingly fluid in appearance, thread their way through the barren earth. More than 250 years ago Lanzarote experienced the Story of the Creation again. In the Timanfaya National Park, home of the Fire Mountains, are so called "moon-scapes". From these one can really get an idea of the "sea of silence" and the powerful forces which are massed and captured beneath the earth's surface. Yet the mountains give a tranquil impression, as though little villages were buried beneath them. Here and in other parts of the island art has been made without artists and the landscape has been sculpted without landscape architects.

Nature bequeathed the area with bizarre sculptures, painted the stage sets and wrote its own dramatic script. The island's many con-trasts are a constant source of excitement. The whitewashed houses, the black fields covered with *picón* (a volcanic rock and granules of lava), planted with corn and onions. Lime green, yellow, tomato red against a dark background. A dromedary draws the plough, the *magos* (farmers) still harvest together, from field to field. Solitary palm trees, their plams softly curling over to form a shady roof. The softly sloping mountains change their colour according to the light. He who seeks it, can find surrealism "in real life". Natural stone walls thread their way through the planes. Wine and figs thrive in the man made craters (La Geria).

It is worth taking a walk along the west coast. On some days the on shore winds throw up rainbows in the spray. Sharp-sided blocks of magma stand out, giving the impression every now and again of figures.

Then there are the white beaches in the south – Papagayo – they are still protected against property development, but the crowds have long since arrived. They are the island's most beautiful beaches.

Lanzarote has no woods, very few springs and no ground water. The Harmattan, Sirocco and Levant are all desert winds which have brought sand from the Sahara, which, in turn, creates new deserts. But in earth can flourish. Poppies and daisies and much besides grow after infrequent rain falls (predominantly in winter).

He who visits at any time apart from high summer can find surpringly sumptuous vegetation in the north. This is especially surprising for this dry island. Haría is a good example. In the valley of a thousand palm trees, a grove houses a village with a strong Moorish flavour.

Lanzarote possesses elemental force and aesthetic power. The architecture was adapted to the landscape. A solitary tower block in the capital Arrecife acts as a warning against high rise developments. The tourist trade was concentrated on three villages: Puerto del Carmen, Costa Teguise and Playa Blanca.

The people of Lanzarote are unassuming, hospitable people; they are slightly reserved, but their reserve has nothing cold about it. They have a happy disposition, one can see that they work hard, that the older people have known deprivation; that makes them tough, but not hard. Lanzarote, known of old as Tyterogakaet, Tyteroygatra or Tarakkaut is the most north easterly, the strangest, most original and impressive island of the whole archipelago of the Canary Islands.

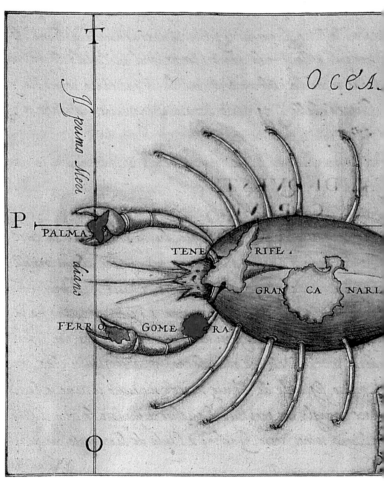

Canarias under the Sign or Cancer by Leonardo Torriani, 1590, original
30.8 × 18 cm, coloured, reproduced by kind permission of the Colegio de
Arquitectos de Canarias, Demarcación de Tenerife, La Gomera y El Hierro,
Archivo Histórico.

ATLANTICO

Turueueo

Allegransa
S. Chiara
La Gratiofa.   Roccha del lefte.

Mefta.
Algrancin

LANÇAROTE.
Isola de louos.

C. Sonca.

ATLANTE
MINORE

Deno.

L

FORTEVENTVRA.

S. Bartholameo

PARTE DELLA MAVRITANIA

9

I
AT THE TROPIC
OF CANCER –
ON THE CANARY
ARCHIPELAGO

1.
MYTHOLOGICAL
BACKGROUND

The Canary Islands. Situated on the Tropic of Cancer. The archipelago of eternal spring. The Elysian Fields. The Garden of the Hesperides. The island of the Saints. According to the tales of Herodotus, in whose time the earth was still thought to be a disc, its edge signalled by violent waves, writhing above seefarers, the point where the world ended and the seas were no longer masterable. Here at the end of the inhabited world; the islands of eternal luck, the "Purpurariae", Atlantis.

Towards the end of the 8th century BC Homer wrote of the Elysian Fields in his Odyssee; these were interpreted as being the Canary Islands. Herodotus (around 490–425/420 BC), the founder of greek historiography spoke of the Garden of the Hesperides. According to the myth, it was Atlas', the ruler of Mauretania's, cone-shaped mountain which bore the weight of the firmament. Hesperia bore him seven daughters, called the daughters of Atlantis or even the Hesperides. They were banished from the islands, where they are said to have invented night to protect their golden apples from thieves. It was also thought that Plato's (427–347 BC) sunken Atlantis, described in the dialogues "Kritias" and "Timaios", had been discovered here. In the book of Genesis and the book of Ezekiel the Bible calls the islands Elysa or Elysis and the crimson isles. The philosopher and historian Plutarch (around 50–125 BC) spoke of the Islands of the Saints in his "Life of Sertorius". In the year 24 AD the Mauretanian King Juba II sent out an expedition to discover more about these islands shrouded in legends, but the reports of it have been lost. In the texts of the Roman author Elder Pliny (in the first century AD) – who had never actually seen the islands – one finds the first details of the vegetation. He wrote of dragon trees and pine woods. He named the archipelago the "Purpurariae", an allusion to the purple dye the islands produced, just as, long before him around 1100 BC, the Phoenicians had. They set off from Gades, today's Cádiz, on a voyage of discovery along the Africal coast, came across Lanzarote and Fuerteventura and took from there the Orchilla lichen *(Roccella tinctoria)* from which they gained crimson. The Carthaginians also visited the islands. Despite the numerous visitors, the Canaries were forgotten at the beginning of the early Middle Ages, as early as the 2nd century AD the mathematician, astronomer and geographer Ptolemy (around 85–160 AD) took the island of El Hierro, the island the furthest from the sunset, in the *Punta de Orchilla,* for his prime Meridian. He thus integrated the Canary Islands into the first latitude and longitude grid of the inhabited world and it was only later that the prime meridian was moved to Greenwich. Thus, under the name of *insulae fortunatae* the Canary Islands were part of a world map long before they fell into obscurity.

It is uncertain where today's name for the archipelago comes from. In old writings the island of birds *Canora* (lat. canere – to sing) was mentioned. It is more likely that *Canaria* comes from the tall dogs, which the discoverers found here (lat. canis – dog): thus island` of dogs.

Top: Original inhabitants of La Gomera after Leonardo Torriani, 1590, original 30.6 × 17.7 cm, coloured; bottom: Original inhabitants of El Hierro, original 30.5 × 17.6 cm, coloured, reproduced by kind permission of the Colegio de Arquitectos de Canarias, Demarcación de Tenerife, La Gomera y El Hierro, Archivo Histórico.

2.
TEMPERATURES
AND LOCATION

The cool Canary stream and the continuous trade winds are responsible for the "everlasting" spring, the mild, settled climate. Pleasant temperatures (average temperature in January 17.5 °C, in July 24.2 °C) are the norm for both winter and summer; on a latitude so near to the equator much higher temperatures are normal.

The Canary Archipelago, the last stop before you cross to America, over 1,600 km north east of the Cape Verde Islands, 1,200 to 1,400 km south east of the Azores, about 1,000 km south west of Gibralter and 500 km south of Madeira, is situated 115 to 500 km away from the coast of North west Africa, by Cape Juby.

The archipelago, which is situated on approximately the same degree of latitude as Florida, the Bahamas, the Sahara and Delhi, comprises seven main islands and six smaller islands. They are divided into two groups: The Fortunates: La Palma, El Hierro, La Gomera, Tenerife and Gran Canaria and secondly the Purple Isles Fuerteventura and Lanzarote. Taken as a whole the islands measure 7,499 square km and stretch about 500 km from east to west (between a longitude of 27°38' and 29°25' north) and more than 200 km from north to south (between 13°20' and 18°9' longitude west. If you catch the passat, so the sailors say anyway, and if you sail unerringly and with the wind, you can reach the Panama Canal from here – at the end of which the Galápagos Islands are known to be.

3.
GEOLOGICAL
ORIGIN

Are the Canary Islands the remains of a sunken continent? Are they, along with the Azores, the Cape Verde Islands and Madeira the last and thus the highest elevations of Atlantis? Atlantis, which according to Plato was bigger than both Asia and Libya together, is said to have been engulfed by a flood in one night; the flood is said to have been caused by the development of a moon.

The theories about the geological origin of the islands are contradictory. Going by current research, the search for Atlantis here seems to be mere illusion. Moreover, the theories that the islands and Africa were once joined by a thin strip of land or that the Canary Islands were situated on a continental crust have not gained credibility. Today it is supposed that the islands are of purely oceanic origin and were never joined to the continent.

Parts of a volcanic plug were raised thousands of metres tectonically. The structuring phase, known as the shield phase, lasted half a million years and formed 90% of the land. Fuerteventura and Lanzarote are the oldest islands. They came into being in the middle Miocene, about 16–20 million years ago. Gran Canaria is thought to have been formed 13–14 million years ago, Tenerife and Gomera about 10 million years ago. La Palma and El Hierro are thought to be about 2–3 million years old.

The fall in age from the eastern to the western islands is significant. The drop in age concurs with the theory of plate tectonics which says that the oceanic crust is continuously newly formed by basaltic magma. This is why Europe/Africa and the continent of America have been drifting apart at a rate of 1–2 cm per year for the last 9 million years. The upper mantle, about 400 km thick, is formed predominantly from peridotite stone. The firm lithosphere goes down about 100 km below this. Some scientists presume that the lithosphere moves in an easterly direction to the border area with the aesthenosphere, while magma continuously climbs to the earth's surface from stable chambers in the aesthenosphere. In this way the islands are said to have been formed gradually in a western direction.

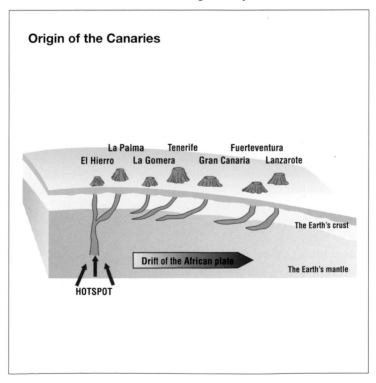

Origin of the Canaries

La Palma   Tenerife   Fuerteventura
El Hierro   La Gomera   Gran Canaria   Lanzarote

The Earth's crust

Drift of the African plate

The Earth's mantle

HOTSPOT

4.
THE ANCIENT CANARY PEOPLE

The first Canary people, the original inhabitants of the archipelago, also known, quite wrongly as *guanches* (*guanches* means sons of Tenerife) were cast up on the islands in about 3000 BC. They probably arrived in primitive boats. Without wanting to. They were probably driven here while fishing off the African coast. They were driven by the Harmattan, the hot Sahara wind, which blows off shore and carries sand and the occasion swarm of grasshoppers with it, blowing in a westerly direction towards the Canary Islands. The Harmattan is accompanied by strong sea currents in the same direction, against which it is impossible to fight in simple boats. Those who went off course and landed on the islands could think of themselves as lucky, although there was no way back.

This theory of origin is thought to be tenable by most scientists today, although no sign of water vehicles from that time has ever been found. Even the architect of the fortress, Leonardo Torriani (1590) supposed that the original inhabitants had reached the islands by boat, possibly in dug-out canoes. This is even more astonishing when one considers that, according to the Spanish conquerors, no connections are supposed to have existed between the individual islands until into the 14th century. So the original inhabitants of the Canaries had no experience of boat building or sea travel. (These reports are contradicted by al-Idrisi, the Arab geographer. In his exposition he claims that 1,124 Portuguese seafarers reported ships that the first inhabitants had used. Anthropological examinations made on skeletons substantiate a possible connection between the islands before the time of the conquest.)

The Spanish chronicles describe the first Canary people as tall, handsome people, some with blond hair, some with red, all with white skin. The Dominican Fray Alonso Espinosa (1594) praised their qualities in his writings. They are said to have been magnanimous, honourable people who kept their word and who were brave, compassionate, never cruel. He also attributes them with great imaginative talents and unusual spiritual capabilities. The race of the first Canary inhabitants is still part of the Canary population today.

The results of anthropological examinations show that the first inhabitants descended from Cro-Magnon people (wide, earthy face), found in western Ireland, Brittany, the South of France, the Basque region and amongst the Berber tribes of North Africa. (Berbers are white skinned, fair or dark haired). The anthropologist Ilse Schwidetzky thinks that the islands were populated at least twice. About a thousand years prior to our calendar, a second Mediterranean type (with a thin, fine face) landed on the islands. Examinations of mummies and skeletons indicate that the Mediterranean type was taller, superior to the Cromagnides and belonged predominantly to the ruling class.

Comparing language and writing, the researcher Dominik Josef Wölfel (1888–1963) discovered some correspondences between the language of the ancient Canary people and North African inscriptions. The spiral stone carvings in the *Cave of Belmaco* on La Palma, the so-called megalithic petroglyphs, a "feeling writing", correspond to discoveries in North Africa, West Ireland and, most of all, the spiral carvings on the Brittonian royal grave of King Gravinius. Inscriptions in Hierro show similarities with Libian and Numidian characters from Punic and Roman times in North Africa and the Tifinagh (the characters) of today's Tuareg (according to Wölfel).

The *Letreros de Julán* on Hierro contain signs of Cretan linear writing. Schwidetzky and Wölfel assume a common source for both writings; they assume it to be the so-called "westculture". (Westculture is a hitherto unknown high culture, which left traces in the Canary Islands and went into ancient Egyptian and Cretan culture.

Original inhabitants, ceramic by Juan Brito

The writings that were found have nothing to do with actual Egyptian or Cretan culture, but, according to Wölfel, are related to the ancient Mediterranean. They have their origins in the pre- and early dynastic age in Egypt and pre and early Minoan times in Crete.) About 1,300 words have been retained from the language of the original inhabitants of the Canary Islands, which, disregarding dialectic differences, had the same origin on all the islands. These words show similarities and uniformities with the language of the Berbers.

The original inhabitants of the Canaries were herdsmen and farmers. They kept mainly sheep, goats and pigs. In the winter they took the herds into the mountains onto the *allmenden* (communally owned pastures). Each tribe possessed a fixed area, often fiercely defended in pastural wars. The arable land was the property of the tribal kings. Families were allocated land for cultivation every year which then reverted to the tribal king after harvest. The size of the plot was determined by the family's standing, the class they belonged to and services to the tribe. The fields were worked upon in groups, which were called *junta* (together) in Gran Canaria, *barranda* or *gallofa* in La Palma.

Usually one group went from field to field, irrespective of who owned what, until all fields had been planted. This custom is still carried out in some of the islands today. Just before the rainy season (around the middle of September) the men began to loosen the earth with wooden furrows, the tips of which had goat horns on, while the women sowed the crop. Barley, wheat, peas and broad beans were grown. After a common harvest the grain was crushed underfoot or with sticks on the *era* (round threshing place). Later the more affluent farmers got their dromedaries and cows to trample the ears of grain, by leading their cattle round and round the era.

The staple diet of the first Canary inhabitants was *gofio*, barley meal that was roasted in clay dishes; today it is still par of the Canary diet (although corn or wheat is now used). The preparation of *gofio* involved grinding grains of barley by hand to a fine flour on lava stone. It was then placed in a *zurrón*, a pouch made of goats leather, and mixed to a dough with some water. Sometimes they used the juice of fruit instead of water or mixed in honey for a finer taste. However, the poor could not afford barley. They had to make do with gofio meal made from bracken roots.

The animals they kept also provided the Canary people with meat, as well as milk and cheese. They had the animals slaughtered – prisoners were forced to do this "degrading" work. Their meals were enriched with figs, dates, and sea food. There is always a large pile of mussels, so-called *concheros*, near the banks of each island, which bears witness to the great consumption of mussels by its inhabitants.

Fish were caught off the coast, without boats and with primitive fishing rods (from wood or bone); they also used lances, fish traps and nets, or more precisely mats that resembled nets, woven out of reeds. In shallow bays – the Canary people could not swim – they drove swarms of fish together. They stunned the fish with the juice of spurge plants, which they shook into the water.

There are plenty of caves and overhanging cliffs of lava and tuff stone on the islands. This meant that the original inhabitants had no accommodation problems. However, strictly speaking, the Canary people were not cave dwellers. If they didn't live in the sparsely furnished caves, then they lived in sheltered ditches or in straw roofed clay huts. This was the case predominantly with the poorer population. They also built huts with skillfully layered walls, built up without mortar. These houses had low doors and small windows and were covered with wooden beams. They covered the beams with straw and laid flat stones *(lajas)* on top of this. Beds were erected from stones; they were also covered in straw, reed mats and animals furs. Mats and animal skins also served as bed covers.

The original Canary inhabitants used tools such as hand mills made from lava which were surprisingly precise, needles and awls made from animal bones and bone gouges, stone knives from Obsidian *(tabonas)*, a hard sharp stone glass, also used for arrow heads. They sewed leather purses and the wrapping for mummies, wove reed sacks, carved combs and vessels out of wood and made pottery of very diverse styles considering the small area.

Wölfel found correspondences to ancient Egyptian and Nubian ceramics in the Canarian tiefstich ceramics. An individual style of ceramics whose ornament was pressed in to the clay was discovered in La Palma. Wölfel claimed the vessels found in Gran Canaria showed parallels with the Mediterranean and Crete in early Minoan times.

Roasting and grinding maize to make gofio

Original inhabitants, ceramic by Juan Brito

The original Canary people wove skirts from reeds and palm leaves; they had no fabric as such. Untanned goat and sheep leather was stitched up with string to form clothes *(tamarcos)*, sandals and the emblems of peasant rebels during their insurrections were made from leather. Jewellery, which also served as a method of payment, was made from slices of clay, mussels, stones and bones and strung together on a piece of twine. Wooden javelins, clubs, arrows and catapults, which they deployed surprisingly accurately, were used by the original Canary people as weapons in tribal feuds and battles against the conquerors.

Battles were led by the tribal king. For the warriors, their leader was their very soul. If the king fell, in most cases the warriors became completely weak-willed. The conquerors soon recognized that they only had to gain control of the headman, in order to vanquish the brave heroic warriors.

A double kingdom was typical of the Canary Archipelago. On Tenerife and La Palma the kings were called *menceyes*, on Gran Canaria *guanarteme*. All kings had advisers and headmen *(sigoñe)* at their side, some islands also had priests *(faican)* and women priests who worked as advisers. When Fuerteventura was conquered two senior women ruled alongside many dukes. The first, called *Tamonante*, had a judicial role, the other, *Tibiabin*, who had medium-istic powers, prophetic power and great knowledge, was a female priest.

Each tribe had a three class system as its basis; first and fore-most king and royal family, then the aristocracy, then the people. Members of the lowest class could be promoted to the aristocracy if they showed special merit.

Only a man of whom no one could say they had seen him milk or kill his goat, steal in peacetime, prepare his own meals, or behave unrespectfully, especially towards women, could be knighted. However, if anyone at the ceremony could claim anything to the contrary, the candidate was relegated to being a common soldier until the end of his days, was completely shorn and was called from then on *trasquilado* (the shorn one). Women from the lower orders could probably only reach the aristocracy by marrying. The wives of the king or the headman had to be aristocratic. Because of this, inter-family marriages were common.

The king's elder brother and then the king's son were next in line to the throne. In Tenerife every kingdom had a living and a dead king. The relic elevated the dead man to the status of a still ruling king.

The marital customs of the original Canarians left them with great personal freedom. If two people wanted to marry, the partners will was sufficient. In the same way a declaration of will by one of the partners was enough to end the marriage. There war no obstacle to getting married again. However, the children of a separated marriage were disadvantaged; they were regarded as illegitimate. There is still debate as to whether the women of Gran Canaria and Lanzarote were married to three or four men, who alternated every month in their role as man of the house and beneficiary of marital rights.

Every island had a different system of penal law. On Fuerteventura the criminal's skull was smashed in with a stone. But the "Sons of Tenerife" were unusually mild. The murderer was relieved of his property (which was given to dependants as compensation), and was then chased out of the kingdom. On Hierro the price paid for theft was an eye. On La Palma, however, theft was regarded as an art.

The original Canary people on all islands believed in a single, almighty, good god by the name of *Abora*, *Acuhurajan* or *Althos* (all three words mean great). *Abora* was the counterpart to *Guayota*, an evil god. He was believed to live in the crater of the Teide on Tenerife and avenge the evil deeds of people with volcanic eruptions. On circularly constructed places of sacrifice at the foot of volcanoes, the faithful tried to appease *Guayota* with gifts.

Consecrated virgins, the *harimaguadas*, who dedicated themselves to the service of *Abora* lived in the caves in the mountains. After a few years of abstinence they were allowed to leave the women's order and get married. The kings and aristocrats had first pick of the virgins. The best known monastery is the site of *Cenobio de Valerón* on Gran Canaria. 297 caves served as monastic cells and granaries; they were joined in seven and more floors by galleries and stairs.

Priestesses had the task of asking for rain and, in times to catastrophe, for *Abora's* protection. The priests, on the other hand, took on a judicial role and acted as a mediator in great quarrels.

The cult of the dead of the original Canary people is reminiscent of the culture of ancient Egypt. The corpses of the upper class were mummified. The innards were removed, but never the brain, all orifices of the body were sealed with bees wax and the body was rubbed with a mixture of animal fats, the sap of the dragon tree, aromatic herbs, resins, tree bark and crushed pumice stone. The drying out process lasted several weeks. The mummies were subsequently sewed into goat and sheeps skin, laid in dug-out tree trunks and buried upright in caves. The mummies had no bandages as was customary in Egypt since the Canarians could not weave. A mummie wrapped in goat's leather can be viewed in the Canary Museum in Las Palmas de Gran Canaria. Members of the lower classes were not mummyfied, but just buried in caves.

Tumulus burials are also known from Gran Canaria (tumulus means prehistoric sepulchral mound). This is mainly represented by single graves. The dead man was laid in a dug out grave and the ground was covered in stones. The big tumulus of La Guancha at Gáldar is still noteworthy. It contains over thirty burials and is estimated to date back to 1082 AD. Due to its climatic conditions, Gáldar was a rich area and the seat of the royal dynasty *Andamanas*, along with the high aristocracy. It is possible that the great tumulus was the grave of this clan.

Apart from natural catastrophes and occasional attacks by slave dealers or pirates, the original Canary people lived for hundreds of years in peace and quiet, forgotton by the rest of the world, engrossed in a stone age culture with little sign of change without knowing about the invention of the wheel and without metal mineral resources. They lived in peace – that is until the Christians came.

The "abandoned" islands found notice once more. And every piece of land where the inhabitants were not Christian was also regarded as "abandoned". In the 14th century the Spanish conquerors showed the original inhabitants what Christian civilisation and brotherly love meant. Under the auspices of the Bible they held in front of them, they struck dead all those who didn't submit. The same fate befell the original inhabitants of the Canary Islands as was to befall the Indian Americans. The conquest of the Canary Islands was a dishonourable and gruesome massacre which took the majority of the original inhabitants as its victims.

5.
REDISCOVERY
AND CONQUEST

The Canary Islands were next discovered by Genoan seefarers in 1292. However, Europeans only developed a real interest in the islands at the beginning of the 14th century. In 1312 the Genoan Lanzelot Maloisel, known as Lanzarotto Malocello, landed on the most north easterly island Tyteroygatra (named by the original inhabitants). This island was probably named Lanzarote after him.

In 1341 the Portuguese king dispatched three war ships which landed on Gran Canaria. Their five month long occupation of a coastal strip proceeded with great losses. With little booty, but taking five Canarians, the unsuccessful conquerors sailed back to Portugal.

Between 1340 and 1342 the islands were plagued by Portuguese, Spaniards, Mallorcans out to catch slaves and involved in robbery.

The nobleman Luis de la Cerda – Count of Talmot, feudal lord of Oléron and of la Mothesur Rhône, Admiral of France, son of the disherited King without land, Alphons of Castile and grandson of Alphons X of Castile – was crowned king of the Canary Islands in 1344 in Avignon by Pope Clemens VI – the head of all countries still to be discovered. For a yearly payment of 400 golden florins to the Roman church, de la Cerda was given the kingdom which he believed he had been cheated out of. Luis de la Cerda never conquered his kingdom. Even an expedition there seemed too dangerous for him. He merely had to defend his distant kingdom against the demands of Portugal and Castile.

Henry III of Castile inherited the islands and nominated Roberto de Bracamonte as de la Cerda's successor. But like his predecessor, Bracamonte could make little of his title. Bracamonte

Castillo de San José in Arrecife

actually did keep the title, but appointed his nephew, the Norman nobleman and knight Jean de Béthencourt (1359–1426) – who had fallen out of favour with his own King Charles IV – to conquer the islands.

In 1402 Béthencourt, together with the Spanish nobleman Gadifer de la Salle (1340–1422), set sail from La Rochelle for the islands. Once they had landed on Lanzarote they converted the chieftain *Guadarfía* and his subjects quickly to Christianity. The natives were saved from slavery by their conquest.

For the first time the Spanish crown possessed one of the Canary Islands. In the same year Béthencourt returned to Spain to request means and reinforcements to conquer the other islands. The diplomat installed the actual conqueror of the islands and warrior La Salle as his representative and governor on Lanzarote. At court in Seville Béthencourt concealed La Salle's victories from Henry III and increased his own excessive levy; this brought him the title of "Lord of the Islands". When La Salle, who had also harboured hopes of the title, heard of Béthencourt's misdemeanours, he returned to France in bitter resentment.

In 1405 the people of Fuerteventura surrendered. This conquest was described by Béthencourt as a *"great adventure" (fuerte ventura)*. In Fuerteventura he founded his capital Betancuria, where the first episcopal church of the archipelago was founded in 1424. He also conquered Hierro, which fell to him through betrayal. *Armiche*, the ruler of Hierro, trusted the word of Béthencourt who had suggested peace talks. The island prince surrendered with 111 of his subjects. Béthencourt seized hold of these original inhabitants and distributed them like animals amongst his people, some were even sold as slaves. Although he has often been accredited with having done so, he was not able to conquer Gomera. Gomera was still counted as the property of the Béthencourts. They sold estates to aristocrats under a feudal system. Attempts to conquer Gran Canaria and La Palma failed. In 1406 Béthencourt returned to Europe and gave the affairs of the crown over to his nephew Maciot de Béthencourt who ruled until 1415 as viceroy.

He ruled unscrupulously and brutally. He lined his own pockets quite indiscriminatingly until finally on the instigation of the Spanish King he was forced to give up his office. In 1418 he sold his office directly on to several people. He sold to the regal envoy Diego de Herrera, to Prince Henry of Portugal and to the Spanish Count Hernán Peraza the Elder.

Hernán Peraza the Younger took over the rule. His heir(ess) Doña Ines – married to Diego García de Herrera – continued the corrupt feudalism until the catholic King Ferdinand of Aragon and Isabella of Castile ended the privileges of the aristocracy, by setting the islands under the power of the Crown.

However, the property laws remained unclear. The Portuguese, for their part, also made claims to the archipelago. A contest between the two royal houses had begun. Attempted conquests by the Portuguese lasted from 1420 to 1479. On Gomera they could assert themselves without subjugating the natives. In the treaties of Alcácovas and Toledo (1479) the two parties came to an agreement: Castile was entitled to pursue the conquest of the whole of the Canary archipelago, while Portugal's supremacy in North West Africa and Guinea was recognized. Colonisation could begin.

In the name of the Castilian crown, Juan Rejón founded Las Palmas de Gran Canaria as early as 1478. Bloody clashes had raged with the original inhabitants for five years. They only came to an end when the Spanish were able to entice the *guanarteme* of Telde, *Doramas* into an ambush, kill him and hang his head out for display. The resistance of *Doramas'* subjects was over. The second king, *Artemi Semidan*, *guanarteme* of Gáldar, was transported to Spain where he was baptized.

Even though the original inhabitants of Gran Canaria rebelled again and agian, the conquistadores celebrated surrender on 29 April 1483. In 1488 Gomera fell, in 1496 La Palma. By the end of the same year the Spanish also had the upper hand on Tenerife.

The aristocratic Andalusian of Galician descent Alonso Fernández de Lugo and the conquistador Pedro de Vera broke the resistance on Gran Canaria and La Palma. After months of fighting they offered the Canary people a cease-fire. The Spaniard's lack of dignity again became evident: they broke their word and took the leader, Prince *Tanausú*, captive on his way to negotiations. At this point, as on Gran Canaria, the original inhabitants surrendered. *Tanausú* brought his life to an end with a hunger strike.

On Tenerife the *guanches* were able to defend themselves more successfully at first. Admittedly, the nine ruling *menceyes* were constantly feuding so that the *mencey* of Güimar, *Añaterve* allied himself with Lugo against the other chieftains, yet the *guanches* inflicted a painful defeat upon the Spaniards. The *guanches* were led by *mencey Bencomo* of Taoro (Orotava Valley) and his brother *Tinguaro*. In spite of their superior weapons, over 1,000 Spaniards fell in 1494 near today's village of La Matanza de Acentejo (the slaughter of Acentejo).

A year later, in a last battle, the *guanches*, weakened by a European plague which the conquistadores had brought in, were devastatingly defeated near La Victoria de Acentejo (the victory of Acentejo). A year later the last *mencey* surrendered.

From now on the Spanish had the archipelago firmly in their grasp. There is still an independence movement today, which a strong minority of the Canary people belong to.

6.
COLONISATION

In 1496 de Lugo founded the city of La Laguna on Tenerife as the royal seat and administrative capital. The Spaniards seized hold of the fertile valleys in the north of Tenerife and drove the *guanches*, the actual owners of the land, to the barren south. In the following period the original population was integrated into the class of the Spanish conquerors – as long as they weren't sold off as slaves, that is. Spaniards married Canary women. Over the next centuries the peoples interbred.

La Palma, Gran Canaria and Tenerife, the profitable "green" islands were directly under the authority of the Spanish crown after the conquest. They were called *islas realengas* (the royal islands). The *capitanes generales* (general captains), the military commanders of the provinces, possessed the highest authority, together with the leading representatives of the catholic church. The general captains gave out the usufructs for the land and sold the water rights.

Gomera, Hierro, Fuerteventura and Lanzarote, the "dry" islands, were also under the authority of the crown, but also received *señorio*-status; that is the property rights were given to the aristocracy and clergy, the *señoriales*, the feudal lords. Their land was tended by slaves and bondsmen or was leased out to *medianeros*. The owner and the leaseholder shared the net profit exactly between them *(en medio)*.

Sugar cane plantations were planted, trade was done with wine and pot herbs. Travellers to America stopped off here, the first riches were gained.

It was primarily the foreigners who pocketed the profit. They possessed the water rights, the land, the plantations and some of the

Corpus Christi in Orotava on Tenerife

ports. Speculating Italians, Spaniards, Dutchmen, Englishmen and Frenchmen were the major participants in the "capital investment" of the Canary Islands. The original Canary inhabitants and their country were relentlessly exploited. The *godos*, the exploiters, who were already rich, became richer; the majority of the original inhabitants of the Canaries, however, remained poor. The sums they invested were always lower than the sums that the speculators and tradesmen transferred abroad.

In 1537 the Spanish crown finally banned slave trade. Despite this, the profiteering conquerors repeatedly broke this ban. A recent decree by Pope Paul III made slave trading punishable.

The Canary Islands won increasingly in strategic and economic importance; more and more ships stopped in their ports. Hundreds of visitors visited the islands, some of them undesirable.

Pirates were attracted by the promise of a keen booty, the archipelago became a renewed target for conquests. In 1599 a Dutch fleet landed off Gomera. After England had won authority of the seas, they repeatedly tried to capture the islands for their empire. In 1657 the attack by Admiral Blake was fended off. During the Spanish War of Succession the attempt by Admiral Genning, who in 1704 occupied Gibralter for England, to conquer Santa Cruz de Tenerife failed. In 1797 Admiral Horatio Nelson, who later won at Trafalgar over the Franco-Spanish fleet, threatened Santa Cruz with a fleet of eight war ships.

With his crew of 1,200 he at first succeeded in going ashore. However, when the defending army received reinforcements and aimed their fire at the ships, Nelson was forced to weigh the anchor and turn about. The Spaniards sunk the auxiliary cruiser Fox and its crew of 200. In this act of conquest, the victory veteran Nelson was hit by a bullet. Using a saw and much rum for anaesthetization his right arm was amputated. It was only after Nelson had signed a pact of non attack with his left hand that the commander of the Spanish fortress Antonio Gutiérrez released the English prisoners. The El Tigre cannon in the harbour of Santa Cruz is still today a memory of Nelson's only capitulation.

Santa Cruz de Tenerife had already become the administrative capital in place of La Laguna in 1723. In 1778 it was given the privilege of being able to trade with America.

7.
INTO THE
20TH CENTURY

I n spite of their strategically favourable situation, events of world history in the 19th century made no impact on the Canary Islands. In 1822 Santa Cruz de Tenerife was made into the capital of the whole archipelago. In 1837 the *señorio*-status was abandoned on Gomera, Hierro, Lanzarote and Fuerteventura. In 1852 the Spanish queen Isabella II made the Canaries into a free port zone. Towards the end of the 19th century the export-oriented banana production became the main branch of the economy.

In 1912 the *cabildos insulares* were created; a local self governing body, a form of state parliament for each island. And in 1927 the archipelago was divided into two provinces; the province of Santa Cruz de Tenerife with the islands Tenerife, Gomera, Hierro and La Palma, and the province of Las Palmas de Gran Canaria, with Gran Canaria, Fuerteventura and Lanzarote.

Both provinces formed a communal military area under the control of General Francisco Franco. In 1936 in the Esperanza wood on Tenerife he gathered together the leading officers and called for

Lago Martiánez in Puerto de la Cruz, Tenerife

a "national uprising" against the Republicans. This resulted in the Spanish Civil War in which German socialists and communists fought on the side of the Republicans whilst Franco was supported by Hitler's troops. The Civil War raged for three years ending in victory for Franco. Franco remained the dictator of Spain until his death in 1975.

On 22 November of the same year King Juan Carlos took over power as the head of state. In a parliamentary monarchy the parliament, the Cortes, adopted a new constitution in 1978. Spain became a consitutional monarchy. Five years later the Canary Islands, like the other sixteen "Autonomous Regions" received a regional constitution (statute of autonomy) and elected representative bodies. Spain's membership of the European Community followed on 1 January 1986. However, the Canary Islands won a special status.

Tourism on the Canary Islands holds a special place today. Contributing 67% to the gross national product, it is the most important branch the economy on the archipelago. Since 1955, when the fishing village of Puerto de la Cruz on Tenerife began to develop into one of the leading tourist spots in the world, tourism has grown constantly – with only occasional breaks.

8.
QUOTES FROM
28 CENTURIES

But you, O beloved of Zeus, Meneleus, are not fated
To die in the steed feeding Argos,
You will be led by the Gods once to the ends of the earth,
Into the Elysian Chamber, where the burnished hero Radamanthus
Lives and peaceful life is the constant comfort of mankind:
(No snow is found there, no winter hurricane, no pouring rain,
Eternal blow the rustlings of the lightly breathing West,
Sent by the Ocean to softly cool humanity) …"
HOMER, The Odyssee, 8th century BC

There are two of them, divided from one another by a very
narrow stretch of sea, ten thousand leagues from Africa; they are

called the Islands of the Saints. Watered only infrequently by mighty falls of rain, mostly by gentle dew-bringing winds, they offer not only a good and sumptuous land for tilling and planting, but also bear exotic fruits, sufficient in quantity and taste to feed an idle people without work and troubles. The climate on the islands is very pleasant resulting from the mixture and hardly noticeable change of seasons. The North and East winds blowing from our part of the world scatter when they reach this breadth of endless space and become weaker; the sea winds blowing up from the South and East sometimes bring mighty rain storms from the sea, but mostly they shower the islands with a moist breeze which makes them fertile. It is for this reason that the firm belief has spread as far as the Barbarians that this is the home of the Elysian Fields and the Saints, about which Homer had waxed lyrical. *PLUTARCH, Comparative Descriptions of Life: Sertorius, 1./2. century AD*

"(…) Today we were able to put into Gran Canaria. I was frustrated in my hope of replacing the "Pinta" by another ship. So we have no option but to try and get a new rudder made. Pinzón thinks he will manage it. I would also like to replace the triangular sails of the "Niña" with round ones, so that the ship can work more securely and won't have to stay behind. For the seefarer there is no greater enemy than superstition. As we passed Tenerife we were able to observe a volcanic eruption in process. The smoke and the flames, the glowing masses of lava, the muffled din coming from the earth innards, put the crew into a panicridden dread. A bad omen – what else? I told them of Etna and other volcanoes, but my words fell on deaf ears. They believed that the volcano had only erupted because we were making this trip. I was certainly concerned about this, but even more disturbed by the news that a ship coming from Ferro" (Hierro today) "brought. Apparently there are three Portuguese caravels at sea with the task of taking me captive and bringing my expedition to an end. The passage from La Rábida to Córdoba is long and that from Palos to Lisbon even longer. Nevertheless, the King of Portugal knows very well that I have gone to sea. He no longer needs me, now that Diaz has found the Eastern passage to India; nevertheless he wants to deny me the western passage. If I succeed – and I will succeed – in winning the seas and reaching areas where no other dares to go, Joao's caravels will return to Lisbon empty handed. Time which previously always passed too quickly, is now passing too slowly. The "Pinta" will not be sea worthy for another three weeks." *CHRISTOPHER COLUMBUS, Log-book, 9 August 1492*

"There are two wheat harvests, one in February and one in May. The grain is uncommonly good and produces bread which is as white as snow (...) This island produces particularly fine wine, predominantly in the town of Telde, and particular sorts of good fruits, the best of which is definitely the plantano. The tree provides no domestic wood; it grows near to the streams, the stalks are very thick and it has an extrordinarily thick foliage which grows not from the branches, but from the top of the tree. Every leaf is two cubits long, and almost half a cubit wide. Each tree has only two or three branches and on these the fruit grows – thirty or forty more or less at a time. The fruit looks like a cucumber; when it is ripe it is completely black and much tastier than any preservative. This island is also the home of many oxen, cows, camels, goats, sheep, capons, hens, ducks, doves and partridges. Wood is the thing which is missing most." *THOMAS NICOLS, Description of the Canary Isles, around 1560*

"It is only in the last 120 or 140 years that the Canary people have known illness; they lived without knowing or feeling it before. If this state of health can be attributed to the completeness and mildness of the air, the reason for it must also lie much more in their little varying and complimentary diet; they feed on only barley, cooked, steamed or roast fish, milk and butter – substances which are good for human health. (...) Since the Canarians have been living in peace under the rules of kings, they have begun to build houses and settlements together and have got used to living in an urban environment abandonning their lives as farmers and herdsmen. (...) The Canary people also built houses in the caves of mountains or dug out the tuff or solid earth – all this without wood or iron or other tools apart from goats bones and very hard stones which could cut the finest and sharpest steel. They made the stones so fine and smooth that they could even use them to bleed themselves and they are currently used by farmers in Canaria as razor blades, called Tavas, just as they were once named. (…) Amongst these Canary people there were three types of fights for which they had three different sorts of weapons. The first two are mentioned above, the third was those thin stones called tavas they used for cutting and bleeding themselves. They used these to injure each other when they fought breast to breast. When two Canarians challenged each other to a fight, they went to the appointed place, a small raised area with a flat stone on either side, just big enough for a man to stand upon. Firstly, each man stood upon his stone with three pebbles in his hand to throw at the other, those three stones used for injuries and with the stick called a Magodo and Amodeghe. First of all they threw the stones at each other, which they skillfully avoided without moving their feet. Next they stepped down onto the ground and encountered each other with clubs, each one fencing and looking for an advantage, in the usual style of fighting. And then, in the full fury of the fight, if it came to a scuffle, they used the three sharp stones which they had between the fingers of their left hand to injure one another. And then one of them proclaimed himself beaten by the other by crying in a loud voice "gamá, gamá" meaning "no more, no more", upon which the victor stopped fighting and the two became friends with each other. *LEONARDO TORRIANI, The Canary Isles and Their Original Inhabitants, 1590*

"Anderson, the natural scientist on Captain Cook's third expedition, advises European doctors to send their patients to Tenerife – not because some healers perversely choose the most remote resorts, but much more to do with the extrordinarily mild and even climate in the Canaries. The island is built like an ampitheatre and, as with Peru and Mexico, although in smaller measures, displays a range of climates from African heat to the frost of the high Alps. Santa Cruz, the port of Orotava, the town of the same name and Laguna are four places where the middle temparatures decrease respectively. Southern Europe does not offer the same advantages, for the change of seasons makes itself much too noticeable. Tenerife, on the other hand, both the gateway to the Tropics and just a few days journey from Spain, displays a great deal of the natural magnificence found in countries between the tropics. Several of the most beautiful and splendid forms of the vegetable kingdom can be found here, bananas and palms. He who has an eye for the beauty of nature, can find an even more powerful means of convalescence than the climate. No other place in the world seems more suited to me to rid melancholy and restore peace to a deeply troubled nature than Tenerife and Madeira. (…) Date palms and coconut trees adorn the banks of the sea; high up above, bushes of bananas stand out against dragon trees, whose trunks really do reveal a snake's body. The slopes are planted with vines which entwine themselves around very high trellises. Orange trees covered in blossom, myrtles and cypress trees surround chapels, erected on free-standing hills with reverence. Everywhere property is enclosed by hedgerows of agave and cactus. Numerous cryptogamic plants, especially ferns, clothe the walls, which are kept moist by little clear springs of water. In winter, when the volcano is covered with snow and ice, one can enjoy an eternal Spring in this part of the country. (…) Climbing the volcano of Tenerife is not just attractive because it offers such rich material for scientific research, but rather because it offers he who has a sense for the greatness of nature a wealth of pictorial splendour. (…) On the top of it one not only gains a magnificent view right across the sea, stretching over the highest mountains of the neighbouring islands, but one can also see the forests of Tenerife and inhabited strips of coastal land which appear so near that the outlines and colours stand out in the most glorious contrasts. We settled ourselves at first on the outside edge of the crater and looked north westerly where the coast is dotted with villages and hamlets. Pockets of mist, swirling continuously around our feet, driven by the wind, offered us the most diverse spectacle. An even layer of cloud between us and the lowest regions of the island was punctuated here and there by little streams of air, sent up by the earth's surface warmed by the sun. The port of Orotava, the ships anchored there, the gardens and vineyards around the town were made visible through these openings, which promised to open up at any moment. From these remote regions we looked down upon the inhabited world; we took delight in lively contrast between the arrid flanks of the volcano, its steep slopes covered in clinker, its plateau, void of all vegetation, and the laughing sight of the developed land; we saw how the vegetation divided itself into zones according to the decreasing temperatures as the height rose. Beneath the piton lichen begins to spread over the clogged, gleaming

Christopher Columbus

lava, a species of violet (viola cheiranthifolia), closely related to the viola decumbens, grows along the slope of the volcano to a height of 3,390 meters. Blossoming retama bushes adorn the small valleys, ravaged by rain storms and blocked up by secondary side eruptions. Below the Ratama the area of ferns begins, below this grows tree-like heather. Woods of laurel trees, rhamnus and strawberry trees are situated between the heather and areas planted with vines and fruit trees. A carpet of rich green spreads its way from the areas of gorse and alpine herbs up to the groups of date palms, muses, their feet seemingly lapped by the ocean. The fact that the villages, vineyards and gardens seem so close from the top of the volcano, has a lot to do with astonishing clearness of the air. In spite of the considerable distance, we could recognise houses, tree trunks, the ships' rigging; we could also see the rich vegetation of the planes in the livliest colour. The splendour of the landscape below the tropics is based on this clearness; it accentuates the gloss of the colours in the vegetation and increases the magical effect of their harmonies and contrasts. We extended our stay on the top of the volcano, waiting in vain for the moment in which we would be able to see the who archipelago of blissful islands. At our feet we saw Palma, Gomera, and Gran Canaria. The mountains of Lanzarote which had been free of cloud at dawn, soon shrouded themselves again in thick clouds. The cold temperature that we experienced on the top of the volcano, was very significant for the time of year. In the shadow the thermometer showed 2,7 degrees Celsius. The wind was from the west – that is from the contrary direction to the wind that blows hot air over Tenerife for a large part of the year and which rises up over the burning deserts of Africa. *ALEXANDER VON HUMBOLDT, From Orinoco to the Amazon, 1889*

"The world lives from the Islands."
CÉSAR MANRIQUE, 20th century

9.
FAUNA AND FLORA

In contrast to the vegetation, there are not many different species of fauna on the islands. The wild dogs – from which the name of the archipelago is supposed to be derived – are of course not here any more. Today the *podenco*, the Pharoah dog is bred and used as a hunting dog for small game. It has long legs, with a long pointed snout, pointed batlike ears. Its coat is short in different tones of brown. It resembles the Arabian greyhound.

Donkeys and mules are used as pack and draught animals, in the eastern islands dromedaries are also used. There are herds of goats and – rather more infrequently – sheep on all the islands. The muflon (a kind of mountain goat) is peculiar to Tenerife and La Palma.

On Fuerteventura the striped squirrel is threatening to become a regional nuisance. Apart from rabbits, bats and hedgehogs there are not really any larger wild animals. There are no poisonous snakes and dangerous insects on the island.

There are many endemic species of insects for insect lovers. The brimstone butterfly and the red admiral are the most conspicuous of the butterflies.

The Canary Islands are a winter stopping place for migratory birds. Here you can watch swallows, swifts, larks, the hoopoe, finches, bitterns, shrikes, stonechats, falcons, bustards, sea eagles, sea gulls, vultures and many other birds besides. Indigenous species include the Canary sandpiper and so-called Canary birds, which are named after the island. They are frequent sight by water or in woods, they are grey-green, and they can sing only moderately well. The splendidly colourful singing bird commonly taken for the real Canary bird was bred in the German Harz mountains.

Something of a living fossil can be seen on the island of Hierro – the 60 cm long lizard *Lacerta simonyi*, which dates from the Tertiary Age. The largest species of lizard is found on Gran Canaria, the *Lacerta stehlinii*. It is endemic to the area and measure about 80 cm. Occasionally a slow worm, the small European legless lizard, can be spotted. Because of their shape they are often mistaken for snakes.

The flora on Lanzarote is very varied and it is not possible to mention all plants, so we are restricting ourselves to the most important. If you would like more extensive information on the flora, there is an excellent book "Wild Flowers of the Canary Islands" by David and Zoe Bramwell (published by Stanley Thornes in paperback, 1984) which has a great deal of information as well as clear line drawings and colour photographs.

Our brief survey of the fauna is divided into two sections: endemic species – plants which only grow on this latitude and tropical and subtropical plants from other countries. Of the 2,000 species of plants which grow on the Canary Islands, about 30% are endemic.

ENDEMIC PLANTS

CANARIAN CANARIENSIS   *(Canary bell flower)* flowers between January and April, has a gold red bell-shaped flower.

CRASSULACEEN   *(Aeonium)* is a member of the succulent plant family, also known as the house leek. There are fifty different types growing on the islands, in rocky landscapes. The leaves are often edged with red.

DRACAENA DRACO   *(dragon tree)* is amongst the oldest trees in the world and is typical of the archipelago. It is closely related to the different kinds of Yukka and is a member of the lily family. The tree has no annual rings; the age of it can be estimated, rather unreliably, by counting the number of branches, which don't

Tajinaste

Musa cavendishii

Dracaena draco

Phoenix canariens

Pinus canariensis

ntia ficus-indica

Carica papaya

Viola cheiranthifolia

always grow at the same intervals of time. The oldest specimen is in Icod on Tenerife; the inhabitants declare it to be 2,500 to 3,000 years old. "Dragonblood" was used to mummify the dead and in the production of ointments. "Dragonblood" refers to the resinous excretion, at first colourless, which emerges when the tree trunk is cut. When exposed to the air it turns dark red.

ECHIUM WILDPRETII   *(Tajinaste)* only grows in the Caldera de las Cañadas on Tenerife. In June it produces a candle-like sprout, which can grow to a height of 2 m and contains more than 80,000 blossoms.

ERICA ARBOREA   *(tree heather)*, called *brezo* in Spanish, is similar to the heather which grows in the temperate latitude. Growing to a height of 20 m, the trees have white or pink flowers. It grows at an altitude of over 800 m, sometimes only as a shrub or mini-shrub.

EUPHORBIA CANARIENSIS   *(Euphorbie candalabra)*, *cordones* in Spanish, is spurge plant with poisonous juice, the edges are thorny and the trunks grow like pillars.

EUPHORBIA REGIS-JUBAE,   called *Tabaiba* in Spanish, has cactus-like trunks, which resemble pillars and grow to a height of 1.5 m. The shrub is a sort of spurge, its milky juice is poisonous.

LAURUS CANARIENSIS   *(Canary laurel tree)*. On Gomera the trees grow to a height of 20 m. The leaves are pointed and eliptical and are sometimes used as cooking herbs. However, they are not as aromatic as the bay leaf from southern Europe.

PHOENIX CANARIENSIS   *(Canary date palm)* with its slim trunk and branches that curl over it is one of the most beautiful specimens of the palm family. It has spread from the Canaries to the whole of the Mediterranean. It is related to the North African-Arabian date palm, but its golden yellow fruit is not edible.

PINUS CANARIENSIS   *(Canary pine)* grows on all the islands apart from Lanzarote and Fuerteventura. It grows at an altitude of 1,000–2,000 metres and is the archipelago's most important tree. The hard reddish heart wood is used for building. The conquerors cleared whole forests and used the wood for building ships, fueling the sugar refineries or for the resin and pitch available in the trees. The pine tree grows to a height of 30 m and has a large round top. Its pliable needles, which are grouped together in threes measure 30 cm. Water from clouds and mist condenses on the needles and falls as precipitation. Tests have shown that 1,500 more litres of precipitation falls per year and per square km due to the fully grown pines, than in the treeless areas a few metres further away. Hence, the pine trees which need less for their own consumption than they produce, play a crucial role for the water supply.

ROCCELLA TINCTORIA   *(Dye lichen)*, called *orchilla* in Spanish. Was important even in the times of the Phoenicians for its red dye.

VIOLA CHEIRANTHIFOLIA   *(Teide violet)* also called Violeta del Teide or volcanic violeta, it a botanic speciality. It only grows on the dry pumice stone slopes of the Teide up to an altitude of 3,600 m.

PLANTS FROM OTHER COUNTRIES

AFRICAN TULIP TREE   *(Spathodes campnulata)* comes from tropical Africa. From January to May this evergreen bears orangey red bellshaped flowers, which grow in clusters.

AGAVE.   There are various sorts, but they all have the fleshy leaves ending in a long thorn in common. The leaves are grouped into rosettes. The plants sprouts layers (shoots) from its roots and from the stem. After 8–16 years a flowering shoot grows out of the middle. It can grow up to 12 m high and forms a bough at the end where yellow green blossoms grow. In Mexico the PULQUE-AGAVE *(agave salmiana)* is used to make the Pulque drink and the SISAL-AGAVE *(agave sisalana)*, which is grown in South America, and Fuerteventura, for the fibre produced from the leaves. Rough materials are produced from these fibres such as ropes and sacks.

AVOCADO TREE   *(Persea gratissima)* known for its pear shaped fruit, called *aguacate* on the Canaries, they are used for starters and salads. The leaves are evergreen, the flowers whitish yellow, open pinacles.

BANANA   (from the *Musa cavendishii* family), introduced by the Portuguese from Indochina, it is one of the most important cultivated plants on the archipelago and is still imported. It can grow up to an altitude of 300–400 metres. The annual plants forms a clubshaped inflorescence. In 4–6 months the bananas are ripening. One plants weighs about 30 kg. Once the fruit has been formed, the plant dies, but not without producing new shoots. The strongest of these shoots becomes the basis of next year's plant.

BOUGAINVILLEA *(Bougainvillea spectabilis)* the climbing plant which comes from the South Pacific is seen often on the islands. It has yellowish flowers on three upper leaves, which can be red, white, yellow, orange and violet.

EUCALYPTUS TREE *(Eucalyptus globulus)* comes from Australia. There are about 20 different types on the archipelago. Wood and ethereal oils are gained from this rapidly growing tree. Its silvery suspended leaves are formed so that they are not exposed to much sunlight.

FIG CACTUS *(Opuntia ficus-indica)*, also called opuntia, it was introduced from Mexico in the 16th century. Its fruit is edible. Cochineal beetles are still bred today on its green shovel-like leaves. An analine red dye is gained from its larva which is used in the production of lipsticks, for colouring aperitifs and oriental carpets.

HIBISCUS *(Hibiscus rosa-sinensis)*, also called chinese rose mallow, comes from South China and flowers the whole year round. The one-day flowers are funnel-shaped with a far protruding pistil with many stamens. The flowers are red, yellow and pink.

Strelitzia reginae

OLEANDER   *(Nerium oleander)* very poisonous plant, originating from the Mediterranean. This shrub, which can grow to the size of a tree, produces white, red, pink or yellow flowers.

PAPAYA TREE   *(Carica papaya)*, also called melon tree, comes from tropical America and is cultivated for its fine tasting yellow melon-like fruit.

PARROT PLANT   *(Strelitzia reginae)* also called Strelitzia, comes from South Africa and bears a flower which resembles the head of a bird. The flower is blue yellow with some orange and violet. It flowers the whole year round and is popular as a souvenir.

POINSETTIA   *(Euphorbia pulcherrima)* known in Europe as a pot plant popular at Christmas time. It is easily distinguished by its red upper leaves. It can grow to a height of 4 m.

In addition to the Canary palm *(Phoenix canariensis)* there is the cocus and king palm, the washingtonia and other sorts. There are a number of fruit trees such as almond trees, orange trees, lime trees, lemon trees, pomegranate trees. There are also apples, pears, and grapefruit, pepper bushes and cinamon trees. There are solitary cork oaks, ombus, cedars, aspens; more frequently there are mimosas and mock rubber trees.

Euphorbia pulcherrima

10.
THE CANARY CUISINE

I t is predominantly in the simple restaurants and country inns, where the natives go, that you will encounter typical Canary cuisine. The Canary people eat well and plentifully. The owners of many hotels and tourist centres have changed to serving international dishes. The restaurants range from coffee houses to steak houses to pizzerias to gourmet restaurants – in other words almost everything one is used to at home. The quality of the food on offer is very varying.

In a *restaurante* the main meals are offered just as they are here. The restaurants and cafeterias are required by law to hang out their menus with the prices of all food and drinks. They also have to make a form for complaints *(hoja de reclamaciones)* available, which can be filled out in every language and must be brought to the notice of the authorities within 48 hours. The restaurants are obliged to offer a reasonable tourist menu. It is made up of a starter, main course and desert and usually includes a choice of a quarter litre of wine or mineral water. Bars are a mixture between a restaurant and pub. *Tapas* are nearly always available there and a full meal is also often available. Bodegas serve only wine.

A breakfast *(desayuno)* speciality is the *huevo pasado*. It is an egg, put into a ladle and dipped just once into boiling water. Hors d'œuvres *(entremeses)* and desert *(postres)* are usually eaten at the main meals *almuerzo* (lunch) and *cena* (dinner) by the Canary people.

For snacks between meals there are *tapas*, small canapes. Some bars offer a large range, here are some of the best: chicken in garlic *(pollo al ajillo)*, fish in batter *(pescado empanado)*, meat balls *(albóndigas)*, potato omelette *(tortilla)*, tripe *(callos)*, goulash *(esto-fado)*, potato salad *(ensaladilla rusa)*, octopus *(pulpos)*, meat with pulses and tomatos *(ropa vieja)*, chick peas with belly of pork *(garbanzos)*; sometimes also mussels *(mejillones)*, shrimps *(gambas)* and other sea food *(mariscos)* and much more. A delicious and varied main meal can be had by ordering different *tapas*. *Tapa* actually means lid or cover. The notion is thought to have originated in bars which were only allowed to serve drinks. So that hungry drinkers were not lost to restaurants or inns serving food, the owners proffered a *tapa* with every beer *(cerveza)* or glass of wine *(vino)*. They were little plates of olives, goat's cheese or a piece of meat which they placed on the top of the glass.

You can get almost all the drinks that you are used to in Europe. The local brands of beer are *Tropical* and *Dorada*, the wines from the mainland are recommended, for example from the Rioja region, as are the Canary wines, especially those from El Hierro and Lanzarote. The Canarians drink *ron* (a clear white rum) as an aperitif or vin ordinaire. *Ron con miel* (rum with honey) is particularly nice. The national drink of the Canaries, however, is whisky with mineral water.

After the meal one drinks coffee with brandy, aniseed brandy, banana liquer or a *carajillo*. This is a flambéd brandy (sometimes served with sugar, a coffee bean, a slice of lemon, a little coffee liquer or aniseed liquer), which is put out with black coffee. Unfortunately, this fine kind of *carajillo* is rare; in most bars you just get a *café solo* with a little brandy added.

Top: Tapas – goat's cheese, olives and octopus; bottom: a *pilar*

The coffee is dark roasted. An espresso is called a *café solo*, coffee with a little milk is called *café cortado*, *café con leche* is the name for a coffee with a lot of milk. You can usually choose which kind of milk you would like: cow's milk *(leche natural)* or *leche condensada* (condensed milk).

The mineral waters on offer are good (for example *firgas*); it is good idea to drink a lot of water to compensate for the minerals which are lost in sweat. It is not advisable to drink tap water or well water unless it has been boiled beforehand.

The *pilar* is an integral part of every Lanzarotean house. The *pilar* is a cube of muschelkalk and sandstone which has been hollowed out inside. At the bottom the cube has been rounded off. It is hung in a wooden stand, especially made for it. The Lanzaroteños use this stone to collect their well water. The water is purified and enriched with minerals. It slowly drips into a clay cup which stands on a clay saucer, which has a whole in the middle. This is turn stands on a clay jug, which collects the water as it overflows and keeps it cool. It was a custom earlier to take a sip of water from the clay cup before going into a house. Today the *pilar* is almost only used as a decorative relict. And it really is decorative. After it has been in use for a while, adiantum starts to grow on the stone; it grows very quickly and lusciously. With its lime green leaves and stems that appear to be black and lacquered, like Chinese lacquer, it adorns the *pilar*.

One should not pass on the Canary specialities. As a starter *tapas* or a plate of mixed hors d'œuvres are the best choice. The latter usually comprises goat's cheese *(queso blanco)*, uncooked ham *(jamón serrano)*, roast pork *(chicharrón de cerdo*, and *pata de cerdo)*, olives *(aceitunas)* and much more. The *potaje canario* is a good vegetable soup, the *potaje de berros* an excellent speciality. It is made from potatoes, pulses, meat and fresh water cress. Where fish is served, you can usually also find an original fish soup, *sopa de pescado*, which contains just about everything that the fishermen brings ashore.

Fish is served baked *(a la plancha)*, fileted *(filete)* or cooked *(cocido)*. *Papas arrugadas, mojo verde* and *mojo rojo* (also called *mojo picón*) is served with it. *Papas arrugadas* are small potatoes, which are cooked in salt water in their skins and which can be eaten in their wrinkly skins. The mojo is a typical Canary sauce. *Mojo* consists of a lot of garlic, olive oil, wine vinegar, six local herbs, green chilli *(mojo verde)* or red chili *(mojo rojo)*. *Mojo rojo* is very hot. *Mojo verde* is occasionally served with avocado.

If you want to eat fish, it is best to enquire what the catch of the day is. *Cherne* is a typical Canary fish, which is only found in this corner of the Atlantic. The *vieja* (= old woman) is a tasty carp-like Atlantic fish and one of the first fish specialities of the Canary archipelago. It is cooked in its skin and served with oil and vinegar. *Cabrilla* (goat head fish), *pescadilla* (whiting) are delicious, but hard to find. *Mero* (grouper), *Sama* (red brace) and *atún* (tuna) are thoroughly recommended. Sardines feature on nearly all the native menus.

Shell fish and sea food are a little trickier – the amount caught is not early enough to cover local consumption. Much of it is flown in deep frozen and this is particularly the case with squid *(calamares)*, shrimps *(gambas)*, king prawns *(langostinos)*, cray fish *(langostas)* and lobster *(bogavante)*. The mussels *(mejillones)* are guaranted to come from the African coast or from the Spanish main land. *Lapas* (limpets), which are caught on Lanzarote's cliffs are fresh, of firm consistency and are often served with *mojo verde*.

Caldo de pescado is a fish stock – not a soup – made with freshly cooked fish, which is served with sweet potatoes. The *sancocho* is a genuine fish dish. *Sancocho* is made from simmered dried cod with sweet potatoes, with onions and garlic. The *cazuela* is a fish stew made from filets of fish, tomatos, with onions, garlic and parsley. The south is usually associated with *gofio*. *Cazuela de mariscos* is a sea food stew.

Gofio was handed down from ancient Canary times and means bread. It is made of roasted corn-, barley- or wheat meal that is put into a goat's skin *(zurrón)* with a little water and kneaded. The *zurrón* is also used to preserve and transport the *gofio*, for example when it is used as food in the fields. A manageable portion is taken from the *zurrón* and it is then rolled back into a ball. *Gofio* is rather dry, therefore the Lanzaroteños drink a lot of wine with it. *Gofio* is particularly tasty when mixed with honey and fruit juice. The natives also serve *gofio* with fish dishes, mix it into fish soups, *gofio escaldado*, or stir it into warm cow's or goat's milk or their *café con leche* as an energy-giving breakfast. Sadly, *gofio* can not be found on many menus.

Puchero canario is an excellent dish, which the natives like to prepare on Sundays or public holidays. At least four types of vegetables are steamed separately in salt water or stock. Different sorts of meat are added to it, such as beef, pork, goat, lamb and game (up to seven different types of meat), resulting in a spicey stock.

Other meat dishes which are recommended are: *carne de cochino en adobo* (roast pork which has been laid in a marinade), *cordero* (lamb) with mint sauce. Baby goat *(cabrito)* is something else which should not be missed. The baby goats are bred mostly on Fuerteventura.

Rabbit *(conejo)* is a further Canary speciality. During the hunting season (first Sunday in August until last Sunday in December: Small game hunting; wild rabbit, wild dove, partridge) the best choice is a wild rabbit *(conejo salvaje)*. It is simmered in a meat stock with herbs, chilli, garlic and saffron. *Mojo rojo* is usually served with it.

A Canary native doesn't go without his desert. He usually chooses something good and solid, if he doesn't immediately plump for *flan* (egg custard) with caramel sauce or for melon. *Torrijas* are corn meal cakes with aniseed and honey. *Frangollo* is a sweet dish made from milk and corn, *bienmesabe* a banana dish with almonds, cocoa powder and whipped cream. *Pudín de queso fresco* is a desert made with goat's cheese and eggs. The *bonbon gigante* really is gigantic, at least in calories. It is made from grated chocolate, which is mixed with egg-yolk in a basin above hot water. If you are looking for something lighter, it is best to order fruit *(frutas)*. Particularly good is the "Canary" banana, intruduced from Indochina. It is a small species of banana *(musa cavendishii)*, which is not sensitive to the weather and is particularly sweet. Figs *(higos)* are served rather less frequently, although they thrive here.

The Canary people eat lunch between 13.00 and 16.00; in the evening they don't usually eat much before 20.00. It is usually noisy and the most important thing is that plentiful quantities of each dish are served up. Everyone can eat what they like; the main thing is that they enjoy it. A lot of wine is drunk with the meal. Toasts are only made on the Canaries at special times of celebration. For that very special inn or restaurant, take a look at the chapter on Towns and Sights.

II
ISLAND OF FIRE AND WIND – ABOUT LANZAROTE

1.
THE NAMING OF LANZAROTE

E ven in ancient times the Tabaiba bush (Euphorbia regis-jubae) grew on Lanzarote. A healing drink was brewed from it. The Romans are said to have known the bush under the name of Sarcocolla (fishlime). In old Spanish Sarcocolla means "Laçarotes". However, it is not certain whether this is the reason why the island has today's name.

One legend attributes the naming of Lanzarote to the Norman nobleman Jean de Béthencourt, who landed there in 1402. When he experienced no resistance from the Canarians on his arrival, he is said to have broken his lance in two and cried "¡Lanza rota!" (lance broken). However, Béthencourt is also said to have spoken Spanish and so it is thought he would not have needed to express himself in such banal terms.

The prevailing opinion is that the island was probably named after the Genoan Lanzarotto Malocello who rediscovered the island in 1312.

2.
HISTORICAL
BACKGROUND

L ittle has been written down about the history of Lanzarote.
The search for sources only brings sketchy material. This has
not least to do with the numerous volcano eruptions which
destroyed villages and the archives which they contained.

The first detailed reports appear after 1312 when Lanzarotto
Malocello landed on the island. The original inhabitants whom he
found there, predominantly of the Cro-Magnon race, had been visited
by various seefarers since ancient times. In spite of the many attacks
by pirates which they had to tolerate, they showed great hospitality.
It is presumably due to this hospitality that there were never any
devastating battles between the conquistadores and the ancient
Canarians on Lanzarote.

The people of ancient Lanzarote were part of a principality
which stretched across the whole island. In contrast to the other
islands, where hostile tribes fought among themselves, the people of
Lanzarote held together. Most women – so it is said – had three to
four husbands who alternated on a monthly basis. The next in turn
worked as servant in the house the woman shared with her current
partner.

In 1377 the Spaniard Martín Ruiz de Avendaño landed. As a
sign of his hospitality, the ruling King Zonzamas put his beautiful
wife Fayna at his disposition; she bore Avendaño the legendary
Princess Icó. Zonzama's son Tiguafaya succeeded him; he was later
captured by slave handlers together with his wife and numerous
tribesmen. Guanarame, another son of Zonzama married his half-
sister Icó.

Icó claimed that their son, Guadarfía, should succeed to the
throne. Legend tells how she was put to a smoke test without which

the other tribesmen refused to recognize Guadarfía's rights. Icó was walled into Zonzama's grave with three servants and the grave was filled with smoke. If she suffocated, then her low origin was proven. However, a cunning old woman had advised her to breathe through a dampened sponge which eliminated the smoke. Icó survived and Guadarfía acceeded to the throne.

In 1402 Jean de Béthencourt conquered Lanzarote. This was the start of the conquest of the other islands. It is presumed that Béthencourt, who landed in Southern Lanzarote with a crew of 63 men, met Guadarfía. Béthencourt and the island prince made a pact. The Spaniards were obliged to build a fort against attackers – like pirates and slave traders – while Guadarfía surrendered himself and his people, as he noted, "as a friend, but not as a subject". The fort was discovered under the sand near the now deserted village of Papagayo, along with the chapel of San Marcial which the conquerors also erected. Today San Marcial is the patron saint of the island.

In 1402, while Béthencourt had returned to Seville to request ammunition and reinforcements for the conquest of the other islands, the previously large population is said to have been decimated to about 300 by pirate attacks and slave catchers. In 1405 Béthencourt conquered Fuerteventura from Lanzarote.

Lanzarote fell into the hands of the Count of Niebla and the Herrera-Peraza family, who governed Lanzarote as feudal lords. The distribution of large areas of land that took place at that time is still in effect today, with just a few exceptions. The system of feoffment was abolished in 1837.

Despite the fact that Lanzarote was able to avoid a battle at its conquest, peace still evaded the island. In addition to volcanic eruptions and periods of drought there were repeated attempted conquests and attacks by slave dealers and pirates. Five extreme droughts, which each lasted more than two years, in the middle of the 16th and 19th century, deprived the people of Lanzarote of even the basics of life. From 1703–1779 the people suffered a continued famine. Lanzarote (and Fuerteventura) were almost depopulated. The inhabitants of these islands fled to Gran Canaria and Tenerife. Many died. Refusing to give up, some returned to their homeland and started basic existence again there.

3.
GEOGRAPHY

L anzarote lies between the 28th and 30th degree of nothern latitude and the 13th and 14th degree of western longitude. Situated 115 km from the west coast of Africa, Lanzarote stretches over 62 km from the Punta de Papagayo in the South to the Punta Fariones in the North. It is 21 km wide.

About 80,000 inhabitants populate an area of 795 square km a medium density of population of approximately 100 inhabitants per square km. If one disregards the uninhabitable wilderness around the volcano, which claims about a third of the whole area (260 square km), a middling density of population of 150 inhabitants per square km emerges. For comparison the population density of other places (all figures are approximate): Fuerteventura 14; West Germany 229; England 375; Norway 13; Spain 80. Around 30,000 people live in the capital Arrecife.

Only about 30% of the land is cultivated and of economic value. In the west and north of the island the coastline is rugged, whilst the east and south coast offer white beaches which are good for bathing and water sports. The highest peak in Lanzarote is the Peñas del Chache in the Famara mountain range in the north; it is 671 m high. In the south the Atalaya stands out 608 m above sea level. It is the "local mountain" of Femés. From the top of the Atalaya, when the weather is clear, one can see over the whole island, which is home to more than 100 volcanoes and more than 300 craters. One also has a complete view of the "volcano wildnerness", which, measuring 260 square metres, makes up approximately one third of the whole area of Lanzarote. This is the site of the Timanfaya range of mountains incorporating the Montañas del Fuego (the Fire Mountains). The Islote de Hilario is the last "active" volcano. This volcanic landscape has been made into a national park.

4.
VOLCANIC ERUPTIONS IN THE 18TH AND 19TH CENTURY

The mightiest eruptions in volcanic history took place on Lanzarote between 1730 and 1736. In this period of time George Washington, first president of the USA and James Watt, the English inventor of the modern steam engine were born, Bach composed his mass in B-minor, Handel his concerti grossi; Gottsched wrote his "Suggestions Towards a Critical Poetics for the Germans", Voltaire his French drama "Zaïre", the 1,062 km long canal between Petersburg (the Baltic Sea) and Wolga (the Caspian Sea) was started (finished 1799) and Hadley drew up his theory of the trade winds. The world only learnt of the monstrous catastrophe on Lanzarote much later. Far away from busy Europe, the pastor of Yaiza, Don Andrés Lorenzo Curbelo, witnessed the eruptions at first hand:

"On the first September of 1730 between nine and ten in the evening, the earth suddenly erupted. In the region of Timanfaya a mighty mountain rose up from beneath the earth's surface. Flames shot up and burned for nineteen days on end (…). A few days later a new maw opened up and furious streams of lava were spat out onto Timanfaya, Rodeo and a part of the Mancha Blanca. The lava streamed across the villages, at first swirling and rapid like water, then heavy and glutinous like honey. With a mighty roar rock emerged from within the volcano and changed the direction of the flow of lava. Now it no longer flowed towards the north, but in a westerly direction. It reached the villages of Macetas and Santa Catalina and completely crushed them under its flow. (…) On the 2nd of September 1731 the lava made a further violent attack. It rained down on Mazo, burned and buried the village and plunged, like a fiery cataract and with the most hideous din, into the sea. This went on for eight days. After this everything became quiet again and it seems as though the eruptions were at an end. But on the 18th October three new mouths broke out directly above the cindered Santa Catalina, emitting clouds of smoke which covered the whole island.

They carried ash with them. Heavy drops of rain fell over the whole island. Darkness, ash and smoke drove the inhabitants of Yaiza and the surroundings away more than once. They returned, however, since no further destruction followed the explosion. Ten days after this explosion the cattle in the entire district fell dead. It had suffocated on the stinking smog. From the 1st to the 20th November smoke and ash were continuously catapulted from the craters. And on the 27th November a stream of lava whirled down the mountain with incredible rapidity. On the 1st of December it reached the sea. Setting as it cooled, it formed an island surrounded by dead fish. On the 16th of December the lava unexpectedly changed direction; instead of running into the sea it now ran in a south westerly direction burning the community of Chupadero and subsequently devastating the fertile plain of Uga. There the lava stopped and cooled. On the 7th of January 1732 new eruptions devoured the old craters. (…)"

The previously fertile land, once known as the granary of Lanzarote, was buried beneath metres of volcanic material in unimaginable quantities. The good people of Lanzarote waited in fright and dread for many days. They hoped that the volcanic eruptions would soon be over. But "on the 25th of December the earth shook more violently than before and three days later the village of Jaretas was burned out by lava and the chapel of St John was destroyed" (Curbelo).

Now the people gave up the hope that the island could ever come to peace. Led by their pastor, some of them fled to Gran Canaria, others to Fuerteventura and Tenerife. A decree by Philipp V forbade the people of Lanzarote, under the threat of death, to leave the island. So some of them remained on the fire-spewing island.

When the earth finally came to peace on the 16th April 1736, a third of Lanzarote was wasteland. Streams of lava had flooded over the plains of Tomara, destroying twelve villages and crushing 420 houses in all.

Scarcely ninety years later, in 1824, the earth erupted for what is until now the last time. The fertile plains of Tiagua disappeared, devoured by streams of lava. These eruptions were not as extensive as those of the 18th century, but they were nevertheless dangerous. The lava was extremely thin and fluid and careered down the valley with great speed.

This "moon landscape" is unique and is a treasure trove for geologists. All the different manifestations of volcanic activity can be seen side by side. Despite the keen research which has been carried out, scientists are still unable to explain why the last two phases of volcanic activity are separated by millions of years.

Top: Valle de la Tranquilidad; bottom: Caldera del Corazoncillo

5.
THE POPULATION

The island and its population is often brought into association with the rabbit: *isla conejera* (conejo – rabbit; conejera – rabbit warren). The natives call themselves *conejeros*, very roughly translated as rabbit hunter.

As on all the Canary Islands, people address each other by Christian name. In the constant battle against nature, they formed a tough and taciturn kind of people who knew how to cultivate the barren earth with their hands, the dromedary and the Roman plough and with trouble and hard work managed to reap the bare essentials from it. Dressed in black and wearing the typical black felt hat, one can still occasionally spot the *mago* (farmer) drawing the plough, while the women sow the crops or plant onions in their ankle-length dresses.

The Lanzarotenos are a people made up from ancient Canary and Spanish influences; every now and again Moorish traits can be seen in the inhabitants, as well as an Egyptian, Berber or Normanic influence; a touch of the Viking can also be seen in the many Canary people with red-blond hair. The difference between the Cro-Magnon and Mediterranean type can still be seen today.

The people of Lanzarote are conservative, reserved, predominantly catholic (Protestants are very few and far between on the Canary Islands), and they are well-mannered. They are tolerant towards the tourists and the foreigners living here.

Administrative and business affairs are conducted in Castilian *(castellano)*, the colloquial language is also Castilian. Influenced by the South American languages, some farmers speak in an almost unintelligible dialect, halves of words are swallowed, and s-sounds left out. In the meantime, an increasing number of Lanzaroteños have learnt to speak German, English or one of the Scandinavian languages.

The growing tourism and europisation has meant that the almost timeless life style of the Lanzaroteños has started to change – whose *mañana* (tomorrow) took so many Central Europeans aback. Daily life has also become busier and more urbane here on Lanzarote.

6.
FIESTA AND FOLKLORE

iesta is certainly no strange word for *canarios*. There are more days of celebration on the Canary Isles than in any other place. During the carnivals and bank holidays many people go out and the flights and sea routes are completely booked. The number of religious bank holidays is roughly the same as other European regions, but the holidays for the patron saints of the islands come in addition. On Lanzarote the whole summer comprises a series of fiestas, one following the other.

15. 5. Uga
24. 5. Montaña Blanca
13. 6. Güime
24. 6. Haría
29. 6. Máguez
 7. 7. Femés (San Marcial del Rubicón,
        patron saint of the island)
16. 7. Teguise; Puerto del Carmen; Tías, Famara,
        Playa Blanca
24. 8. San Bartolomé
25. 8. Arrecife (San Ginés)
30. 8. Haría (Santa Rosa)
 8. 9. Yaiza (Virgen de los Remedios)
14. 9. Guatiza
15. 9. Mancha Blanca (Tinajo)
30.11. Tao
 4.12. Máguez
24.12. Teguise (Fiesta de Rancho de Pascua)

The main days of the Fiesta are given in the table above. Printed programmes are hung in bars and supermarkets for each fiesta. Villages festivals have a religious and folkloric character, but in most cases they have developed into a sort of fair with motor scooters, shooting galleries and sausage stands. The smaller the village, the more original the fiesta. A fiesta has only one main day, but it begins

Fiesta in Uga

about two weeks beforehand. The Lanzaroteños enjoy dancing into the night, until six o'clock in the morning. Singers, comedians and show girls perform at the larger celebrations. The fiestas are closed with a show of fireworks (which are sometimes spectacular) and the *asadero*, a communal meal of sardines which the inhabitants of the village and the surroundings participate in. They gather around small fires, sitting on the ground, grilling fish. Traditionally the fish is donated by the fishermen of the village, the wine by the wealthier residents. Today, this part of the fiesta is organised by the mayor's office.

The statutory and religious holidays are different in some cases from those in Central Europe. Christmas does not have the same value as here (if hey have fir trees at all, then they are imported). On the 24.12, the *canarios* work until evening. They go to Christmas mass, and celebrate Christmas Eve just like New Year and have only one day of celebration at Christmas. New Year is celebrated out on the streets; it is likely and noisy. At midnight it is traditional to eat *uvas de la suerte* (lucky grapes), one for each chime of the clock.

The most important feast on the Canary Islands is *Los Reyes*, the Feast of Epiphany. On each island three kings are met at the harbour. They then make their way across the villages in a festival procession, giving presents to hospital patients and the occupants of

Ash Wednesday, burying the sardine

old people's homes and orphanages. This is the day when Christmas presents are distributed.

The Canary carnival is similar to the carnival in Rio de Janeiro. At Easter, *La Semana Santa*, processions make their way through the decorated streets. Corpus Christi is a delightful celebration to see. The roads in some villages are decorated with salt carpets. Because blossom petals are so rare, the Canarians dye sea salt and lay artificially-made carpets of splendid colours showing pictures and ornaments. After the procession, which runs along these carpets, scarcely anything can still be seen of the various motives. The fiestas are the most impressive showcase for Canary folklore. The character of the people is illustrated by their customs, dances and songs. The strong communal spirit amongst the Canarians and their open way is evident. Some of the ancient customs have survived over the years. They tell stories of folk history in songs and dances, accompanied by the guitar, mandoline, lute and *timple*. The *timple* the predominant instrument in folk music, is similar to the ukelele, except its bass string is in the middle. They are made in Teguise. The Canarian songs and melodies sound, in part, oriental. There are performances of folkloric events for tourists. This is one way of maintaining the traditions, which due to modern media, are now fading into the background.

7.
CLIMATE

On the Canary Islands ice cold winters, rainy springs, very hot and dry summers (as in the Mediterranean) and gloomy grey November days are hardly known. The Canary Islands have a climate of "eternal spring", a settled climate, ideal for convalescence. The average precipitation is about one fifth of that of central Europe.

Lanzarote and Fuerteventura have an even lower precipitation; in Lanzarote the annual amout is about 135 mm, in Fuerteventura 147 mm. Precipitation is concentrated during the months of November and April. Rainfall is higher on the other islands, due to the higher mountains there. Lanzarote's highest peak measures 670 m, that of Fuerteventura 807 m – too low to touch the rain clouds. Sometimes there is no rainfall all year round, sometimes this lasts for several years.

A maritime climate, a climate influenced by the sea, exists up to a height of 200 m; above 200 m the air becomes fresher and temperatures are more changeable. It is at these heights that the wine is grown, at least in Lanzarote. The temperature changes between 16° and 22 °C. The sky is seldom completely free of clouds, July to October is the hottest period, the most pleasant period is between

February and July, the most pleasant month of all is May (subject to change). The temperature of the water taken over a whole year is between 18° and 23 °C.

The following table is an approximation. One must also consider that different climates can be found of on different islands. On the north and west coasts the temperatures are lower and the precipitation is greater.

Table showing the climate in Lanzarote and Fuerteventura

	Average air temp.	Average water temp.	Humidity (in %)	Days of sun
January	15,3	18	81	18
February	15,7	18	82	16
March	16,2	19	80	20
April	17,2	19	81	18
May	18,1	20	81	18
June	19,6	21	80	16
July	21,5	23	80	13
August	22,4	23	79	12
September	22,1	23	81	17
October	20,7	23	82	18
November	18,5	22	83	17
December	16,3	21	84	16

The Canary Islands are suitable for a sunbathing holiday all year round. Their climate is not only due to their situation in the Atlantic and their proximaty to Africa. While the Sahara, where it is unbearably hot and dry, lies just one hundred kilometres east on the same line of latitude, a Mediterranean climate is ensured by the compensatory effect of the wind and water. The middle air temperature are lowered by 2° to 3° compared to those normal on this line of latitude.

By the north east trade wind (north of the equator; south of the equator it becomes the south east trade wind) and the cool Canary stream which drifts to the south or to the south west of the islands. The feeling of heart is appeased by the trade winds. The name trade winds describes those winds on which one can sail to the continent of America.

In the region around the equator the sun's rays hit the earth very directly. Warm masses of air rise up, resulting in a relative vacuum on the ground. Cool masses of air stream into this equatorial depression from the north and south; these are diverted slightly by the friction caused by the earth's surface. They then come as the north east (and south east) trade winds. In the morning trade wind clouds form in the mountains at a height of about 600 m before dissolving in the afternoon. The mountains on Lanzarote and Fuerteventura, however, are too low for the formation of trade wind clouds. For this reason these two islands, compared to the others of the archipelago, have a more pronounced continental climate with less precipitation and greater shifts in temperature.

Cool water which has been lifted by the off shore winds rises up on the lee sides resulting in a layer of cold air at a height of more than 100 m. This acts as a barrier against the layers of hot air from the Sahara. However, occasionally it is extremely hot, mainly in the summer months, due to the Sirocco. The temperature can rise by 14 °C. The air is full of tiny particles of dust, the horizon has a yellow tinge and the sun is a white disc.

The sirocco comes from Africa bringing with it not only heat and fine dirt, but also sometimes swarms of migrant locusts (about 10 cm in length), capable of completely destroying crops. The last locust invasion was in October 1954.

In the winter the trade wind zone, which is dependent on the position of the sun, shifts to the south. The Canary Islands then stand under the influence of rain-bringing atlantic cyclones (a cyclone is an area of low pressure) from the west. These rainfalls, although still rather few and far between, are more than welcomed here.

8.
ECONOMY

The lack of mineral resources and the barren earth meant that Lanzarote suffered poverty for many years. Agriculture and fishing were the main industries in Lanzarote before tourism began to develop there. They also bred stock, although less than successfully.

Admittedly, the mild climate meant that they were able to cultivate most types of temperature zone crops for most of the year, but the fact that they believed in cultivating one crop only repeatedly brought them into economic difficulties. Onions, corn, wheat, barley, forage plants, fruit, pulses (such as broad beans, lentils and chick peas) are grown for local consumption. The most delicious of the crops grown are the tomatoes, new potatoes and sweet potatoes (also known as batatas). The wine which is pressed here is one of the best on the Canary Islands.

Milk, cheese and meat are provided by goats, cow's milk has to be imported. The minimal stock breeding (pigs and game) doesn't even cover the local needs. On the whole agriculture is declining, making up only about 10% of today's gross national product. Domestic food production barely covers 25% of the island's needs.

With the development of tourism and the favourable income it brings with it, it looks likely that only subsidiary farming will exist in the future – pursued continuously over a period of time this can do sustained damage to the landscape. Some fields already lie fallow today. The trade balance has been in deficit for some time with imports, particularly from Spain, on the increase. Products from

Scandinavia, England and Germany have to be imported for the tourist industry.

Apart from construction, on the increase thanks to the tourist boom, industry (25% of the GNP) is restricted to fish canning plants, where tuna is the main fish prepared. Craft objects and embroidery are made by small and cottage industries.

Electricity is produced by means of heat technology; some independent suppliers use solar energy plants or wind mills. Tenerife is the site of the second largest refinery in Spain of the C. E. P. S. A. *(Companía Española de Petróleos, Sociedad Anónima)* oil company. 90% of the fuel is produced there. In addition, a power station on Fuerteventura supplies Lanzarote with electrical energy.

The provision of water has always been a problem for the Lanzaroteños. The water balance determined, and still does determine, the quality of life. Small amounts of rain (less than 400 mm in an average year), which are unpredictable both in timing and quantity) trickle through the porous earth or gather in a few places where costly wells *(pozos)* have been installed over impervious layers of rock.

After heavier falls of rain the water is pumped from large puddles and water holes into tankers and then into large wells. Collecting tanks can be found on some slopes; they have wells built onto the end of them. In the North, near Mala, a disused dam wall is rotting.

Seven *galerías*, natural reservoirs, which are surrounded by layers of impervious rock and which collect rainfall, can be found in the Montaña de Famara. They are opened up by drilling through the rock. Four of the seven *galerías* in the Montaña de Famara have been put into operation. Ten litres of water per second is collected. There is no running ground water on Lanzarote. Previously, in times of emergency, drinking water was transported from Gran Canaria and Tenerife to the island by tanker.

Now, with the growing population and the explosion of tourism, more and more water sanitation plants are becoming necessary. Almost all very large urbanisations have a desalination plant today. On the Canaries as a whole, three quarters of the agricultural products are irrigated artificially. This is not the case on Lanzarote, where unirrigated cultivation is especially common.

74

9.
CULTIVATION OF UNIRRIGATED LAND

The agricultural cultivation of the Lanzarotean earth was always a hard way to earn a living. A lack of water, the scorching sun and the shriveling winds forced the farmers to be inventive. They use the dry cultivation method, called *secano*, which is characteristic of the Canary archipelago.

One form of the dry cultivation method is sand dune culture *(jable)*. A section of sand dunes, approximately three to five metres in breadth, runs across the middle of the island between San Bartolomé and Teguise. The sand dunes rise to a maximum height of one metre. If the sand is not deeper than 40 cm, seeds are sowed onto the sand. The roots of the germinating seeds quickly reach the top soil which lies beneath.

The sand withholds the moisture and the roots can profit from it. To prevent the dunes from drifting away, the sand is weighed down with stones. They have also recently begun to mix the sand with *picón* (a spanish word). *Picón* is a mixture of volcanic materials, rich in minerals, basaltic lapilli and lava granules, which is very porous and has a hygroscopic effect.

Picón is a component of a much more frequent method known as *enarenado* (*enarenar* = to sprinkle with sand). This system of dry cultivation was developed by the Canary people themselves.

It is known as *enarenado artificial* when the covering layer of volcanic material has to be produced. It is this covering which gives the fields of Lanzarote its typical black colour. The fields are covered in about 10 to 30 cm of *picón*. During the day the volcanic covering heats up, at the same time protecting the top soil from evaporation. The *picón* cools quickly at night, increasing the condensation in the layers of air near to the earth. The *picón* lets the condensation through, and in this way the earth remains continuously moist even without rainfall. The lava granules are changed every ten years.

The top layer down to the top soil is removed when seeds are sown. Using a wooden plough which is incapable of making deep furrows, they "scratch" furrows in the ploughland. The plough is sometimes still drawn by the dromedary. When onions are planted from seeds, contrary to the usual process of sowing, the *picón* is not removed, but furrows are drawn in the covering layer into which the seeds are put.

Lanzarote's wine growing region is situated around La Geria. A wide section of the earth between Uga and San Bartolomé became the natural depository for volcanic material. Here the method of cultivation is known as *enarenado natural*. Deep round funnel-shaped holes have been dug out so that the vines can reach the earth with their roots. This method dates back to the 18th century when the malvasia grape was brought here from Crete.

Figs, citrus fruits and almond trees also grow in La Geria. To protect the vines from the drying wind the wine farmers built walls of volcanic stone around the funnel-shaped holes. The whole area of cultivation covers about 3,000 hectares. One vine is thought to bear up to 50 kg of grapes. The amber coloured malvasia wine, with its spicey, dry bouquet, is one of the best wine on the Canary archipelago. It thrives on the low rainfall, powerful sun and fertile volcanic earth. For this reason the alcoholic content is very high and even the light wine is as heavy as sherry. It is said to contain the volcanic power, which the Lanzaroteños once feared. The malvasia wine soon became known in Europe and the New World and it is even mentioned in the works of Shakespeare. It was the preferred wine amongst the royal Spanish families and its main customer was England until it was surpassed by sherry, the wines of Bordeaux, madeira and port.

In the second half of the 19th century many vines were completed devastated by mildew and the exportation of wine was brought to a standstill. Today the wine is distributed almost exclusively on the Canary archipelago. Different vintages of the amber-coloured malvasia wine can be found in Lanzarote's numerous wine presses along with rose and red wines.

10.
BREEDING DROMEDARIES IN UGA

He who observes but casually a dromedary draws the roman plough behind it or how patently it makes its round of the threshing floor, providing the farmer with invaluable help, cannot deny the animal's dignity. The dromedary, which may at first appear ugly and awkward, is a good natured animal. It is attentive and, apart from in the mating season, gentle and tame.

Dromedaries are exemplarary draught and pack animals, they are also good for riding. They are completely at home in the desert, carrying their "larder" on their backs, humps full of fat which keep them going when nothing is available. The dromedary can keep going for up to eight days without food and water and is able to cover a distance of 32 km with a load of 150 kg everyday. Their hard soled hooves and sealable nostrils are adapted to the desert and steppes.

They are not only hard, tough workers (their average life expectancy is 35 years), they also provide milk, meat, leather and hair. The dromedary is a ruminant, its dung makes good fuel.

It is not entirely clear how dromedaries got to Lanzarote from nearby Africa. It is presumed that García de Herrera brought them with him from his African expeditions. The Lanzaroteños began to breed them. Today they are not so successful. Since 1986 the importation of dromedaries from Morocco has been disallowed due to infectious animal diseases there. Many animals were sold and taken back to Africa. Young dromedaries died repeatedly. The largest breeding ground currently possesses over 200 dromedaries.

The female dromedary bears only one child and has to carry the offspring for a term of 12 months. When the young reach two or three it is their turn to be schooled and they are put into use soon after that. Solitary dromedaries are still used to draw the plough, but the majority of these animals from the species of cloven hoofed animals without horns or antlers, carry tourists around in the national park of the Timanfaya.

Crouching on their knees, which are protected by thick skin, they wait for customers. They wear muzzles although they do not bite. The rider sits on a green wooden seat on the left and right of the hump. The dromedary gets up with his back legs first, then the front ones – when it sits it is the other way round – and steadily rocks the rider to the top of the mountain. In the afternoon, when their work is done and they have returned to Uga, they are fed in their *corral*. They are given a rest from tourism each year, when they are driven into the steppes, where they stay for several weeks.

Dromedary riding on Timanfaya

11.
COCHINEAL IN GUATIZA AND MALA

I n the north of Lanzarote, near to the east coast, around and in Guatiza and Mala, the visitor may be surprised to see a number of giant cactus fields, the purpose of which is not immediately evident. The fig cactus or opuntia cactus *(opuntia ficus indica)* grows here. It is one of the classic succulent plants which produce delicious fruit and are often for sale. However, that is not the reason why hectares of the opuntia cactus are cultivated.

The opuntia was introduced in the 16th century by the Spanish conquistadores, but it was only in the 19th century, when the export of sugar and wine declined, that the Spaniards began to cultivate the beetles on the cactus. The cochineal beetle *(coccus cacti)* which, like the cactus originates from Mexico, feeds parasitically on the flesh of the cactus and is no ordinary beetle. It is responsible for the red carmine acids *(cochineal)*, much prized before synthetic dye was developed.

It was the farmers of Mexico who first managed an annual production of about 430,000 kg of cochineal, until other countries (India and Africa) also began to breed the beetle. The cochineal beetle arrived on the Canaries in about 1831. It can be recognised by the white down which covers its body. It is fat and round, its body formed in two parts with a conical shaped head. With its short feelers and thread-like probiscus it guides itself to and feeds parasitically on the flesh of the opuntia cactus. The women farmers are keen to observe that the egg-laying females are evenly distributed on the cacti and that a healthy stream of reproduction can take place. If the weather and climate are good, up to five generations can be bred each year. They are harvested every two to three months.

Neither the male of the species, which dies after mating, not the mother beetle are harvested. It is the larva which is scraped from the

Opuntia shovel with cocheneal lice

cactus; it is then killed in hot water and put out to dry in the sun. The dried larva is then made into a powder. In ideal circumstances 300 to 400 kg of beetles can be harvested per hectare per year.

Production has declined a great deal since the development of synthetic colour, but for the makers of cosmetics, synthetic dye was not a good replacement. The natural colouring is completely unpoisonous and of the best glowing red. Apart from in the manufacture of lipsticks cochineal is also used in Persian carpets. Soft drinks, sweets and aperitifs are also coloured with it. 25,000 kg of cochineal is still harvested per year in Lanzarote. About 140,000 insects have to be dried for every kilogramme; for 25 tonnes 3.5 million larva are needed.

12.
FISHING

In the early morning the fishermen draw out of the harbour, in large and small boats, and spend the day at sea. They work between 12 and 16 hours; sometimes they spend the whole day at sea. Even small boats, which are only suited to one day catches, bring large trawls, although fishing is in decline. Fishing takes place from March to October.

The biggest fishing fleet on the Canary archipelago, with 400 ships, is moored in the harbour of Arrecife. This no doubt has to do with the proximity to Africa. The fishing grounds around Africa are especially rich; however, during a fishing war, like that with Morocco in 1983, fishing there can be very dangerous. In this case the fishing fleet stays in Arrecife harbour. The capital is also the site of the fish processing industry. It is mainly tuna fish and sardines which are canned there.

The following are some of the most delicious fish and sea food; *vieja* (spiny loach), *cherne* (stone bass), *sama* (red brace), *salmonete* (red barble), *dorada* (golden brace), *merluza* (hake), *mero* (grouper), *pescadilla* (whiting), *sargo* (a kind of brace), *cabrilla* (goat head fish) *sardina* (sardine), *tiburón* (shark) – there are no dangerous sharks near the coastline – *atún* (tuna), *bonito* (a mackerel-like tuna), *jurél* (a form of mackerel), *lenguado* (sole), *calamar* (squid), *choco* (a kind of squid), *pulp* (octopus), *lapa* (large limpet), *gamba* (shrimps), *langosta* (cray fish) and *cangrejo de mar* (sea crab).

13.
SALTMINING
OR THE SALINAS
OF JANUBIO

S alt, which was once more precious than gold, has waned in importance on Lanzarote. Since fishing has been in decline on the Canary Islands and most fishermen no longer conserve their catch at sea in salt, but in cool boxes, the salt pans have become uneconomical. The last of the great saltpans still in operation lie to

the west of Yaiza, by Janubio. Other saltpans have been closed like that on the Costa Teguise in the north in front of the Hotel Las Salinas. Some of them fell victim to the tourist industry, for instance the large plant at Los Pocillos, the Salinas de Matagorda, just a few km east of Puerto del Carmen, where tourist centres stand today.

Janubio is a natural lagoon; sea water is pumped into the man made basins, the *cocederos madres*, which are slightly higher. In previous times it was the windmills standing at the edge of the lagoon which kept the pump mechanism going. The salt water remains in the higher basins for two to four weeks – according to the sun's intensity. It slowly evaporates until it is fed into lower, smaller *cocederos*. It remains here for about another seven days until the salt content has risen to 22°. It is at this point that it is actual fed into the *salinas. Salinas* are small basins divided into numerous squares, approximately about two square metres in size. The salt making process comes to and end here. When this sticky mass has crystallised into salt, it is raked together by salt workers for a final drying and piled into small pyramidal heaps.

In earlier times 15,000 tonnes of salt was produced per year, now it is only 2,000 tonnes produced under careful management. A small part of the total production is sold as table salt. At the procession for Corpus Christi, the Lanzaroteños dye their domestically produced salt and artfully formed bright carpets with dazzling patterns are laid along the capital's streets and village squares. The majority of the salt is still bought by the fishermen who use it to conserve their catch. The *salina* owners also sell salt water with an increased salt content, the so-called *salmuera*. It has a salt content of 25°. It is prepared in special *cocederos,* transported by tanker and is used in sardine fishing boats for conservation.

When the salt was exported previously, it was put into sacks, transported to Playa Blanca by donkey-led cart and stored in a specially constructed hall. It took a month to load a ship at anchor – it had to rowed across sack by sack. The working conditions in the salt-pans were always very hard. The feet of the barefoot workers were often eaten away. Many workers became blind in old age because their sight had been damaged by the glaring, reflecting light. Nowadays, the owners of the salt pans have great difficulty attracting labour.

14.
CRAFT AND
SPECIALISED CRAFT

The usual type of crafts, which exist here – with some exceptions – like everywhere else, are not the subject of this chapter. Your attention is drawn to some highlights. There is the grain mill at Haría, which, admittedly, is no longer driven by the wind, but by a diesel engine from the turn of the century. Broad belt of leather drive the grinding mechanism. Roast corn, used to make gofio, is ground here along with other grains for local consumption.

Haría is also the home of the basket weaver Eulogio. Palm leaf stems are lined up along the wall, obviously out to dry. They are used to make large baskets. He weaves bags, hats and footmats from palm leaves, sometimes using straw and cane as well.

The making of the *timple* is one of the specialised crafts. The *timple* is the five-stringed instrument with its bass string in the middle, which is not dissimilar to the ukelele. It is presumed to originate from the time of the conqueros. The *timple* is an instrument typical of Lanzarote, although it is built on all the islands now. In the former capital of Lanzarote, Teguise, three masters of their trade are still working. One of them taught himself how to make the *timple*. He made his first *timple* at the age of twelve for the fun of it, enjoyed it and refined his from *timple* to *timple*. He can tune the instrument, but not play it. It takes him two days to make the instrument. You can find him by taking the first street on the left, where the Palacio Spinola is, from the marketplace in Teguise. His workshop is in the first street to the left.

Specialised craft has been partially influenced by European culture since the 15th century; Latin American elements also played a part later. For instance, this is true of embroidery, which is espe-

Windmill in Tiagua

cially popular on La Palma (figurative or patterned embroidery = *bordado*) and Gran Canaria (open embroidery = *calado*). The rosette embroidery *(roseta)* is famous. Working at home, the women embroider little rosettes, which can either be used as place mats or can be sewed together as covers and table cloths.

Ceramics are a vestige of the old Canary culture. Using techniques handed down over the years, ceramicists are still making vessels without a potting wheel. They smoothe out the tone with stones and bake the ceramics in a sort of bread oven or in the open fire. These "fire ceramics" are perfect imitations of the ceramics of the ancient Canary people. A small house stands on the roof of the Castillo San Gabriel, the Museum of Archeology. This is the show case for the pots, jugs and archaic figures by Juan Brito, the curator of the museum. Brito has made a name for himself as ceramicist and sculptor.

15.
THE NEW ARCHITECTURE OR CÉSAR MANRIQUE

T he Canary architecture is a modest form of Andalusian baroque and it is at its most modest on Lanzarote where poverty was greather than on Tenerife and Gran Canaria. However, this also makes its forms the purest" (César Manrique).

The island in its present form is unthinkable without César Manrique. His influence and work have left their mark on the island's face. The Lanzaroteños credit him with "having made Lanzarote". Manrique was a painter, sculptor, architect (without having studied), ecologist, curator of monuments, town planner, garden- and landscape architect; César Manrique was the most outstanding artistic personality on Lanzarote, in fact on the whole archipelago.

This vivacious, unconventional and friendly man was born on 24 April 1919 in Arrecife. He volunteered to fight on Franco's side in the Spanish Civil War. When he returned to Lanzarote his first successful exhibitions took place. In 1945 he moved to Madrid, where he began to study at La Escuela de Bellas Artes, funded by a scholarship. In 1950 he graduated in fine art and art education. Shortly afterwards he enrolled at the film school, which he quickly left.

In La Era, a garden restaurant in Yaiza, the last evidence of his Madrid school paintings can be seen, three figurative paintings using faience which depict fishing, agriculture and winegrowing.

In 1953 César Manrique began to paint abstract compositions (a virtual revolt in General Franco's Spain) and exhibited a year later with his friends Manuel Manpaso and Luis Féito who shared the same ideas. Manrique went his own way without following a certain

school, avoiding overinfluence by his mentors Pablo Picasso and Henri Matisse.

By the end of the '50s Manrique had made a name of himself in Madrid. Exhibitions followed in the capitals of Europe, Japan and the USA which led to international repute. He received prizes and was selected for the first time for the Venice Biennale; four years later he was re-selected.

In 1963 his girlfriend and life companion, with whom he had spent 18 years, died. This painful experience was probably the impetus behind his move to New York two years later, where he had been offered a post at the International Institute for Art Education. A few weeks after his arrival he was taken on by the gallerist Catherine Viviano. Suddenly César Manrique was hanging alongside his famous co-patriot Joan Miró and next to Max Beckmann.

In 1968 Manrique travelled directly from New York to Lanzarote, which he found much as he had left it. He had the feeling that the island needed him. He made himself into its advocate and was made its advocate. The fact that many of Manrique's ideas were realized owes much to his indefatiguable energy, his persistence, his expertise and not least the degree of international celebrity he enjoys. He propagated a form of elite tourism, felt "bound" to help the poverty stricken island where the population was supposed to be evacuated 50 years before.

Manrique dreamed of "a paradise for the few who have an eye for the special". His dream failed. But he skillfully carried through his building plans with his old friend José Ramírez Cerdá, president of the Cabildo Insular at that time. Luis Morales, who also worked at the Cabildo, provided Manrique with a congenial partner. Working as a site foreman, he understood how to put Manrique's ideas into practice.

Manrique never drew any plans. He designed the buildings and details on the spot, mostly orally, sometimes he made a sketch on a serviette or made a chalk drawing of the ground plan on the earth. This was the case with the restaurant building at the Castillo San José. For Manrique the key lies in the open country. He had to draft plans, abandon them or correct them on the very site, not in the studio. This was a daring process. Manrique did not need the security of a plan, he exposed himself to an open creative process, which can fail at any time. Building plans were often only signed and approved afterwards long after the last handshake had already been made.

These are just a few of his buildings: the Castillo San José in Arrecife, the Fertility Monument in the geographical centre of the island, Mirador del Río on the steep north bank, the airport at Arrecife, Los Jameos del Agua on the north east coast, the Hotel Las Salinas and a complete settlement: Pueblo Marinero on the Costa Teguise, or the El Diablo restaurant on the Islote del Hilario in the Fire Mountains, the Jardín de Cactus in Guatiza and the Fundación César Manrique in Tahiche.

Manrique shaped the architectural policy and his influence can be seen everywhere on the island. He was able to persuade the authorities to inflict a complete ban on advertising hoardings and was made artistic director of the construction company, Río Tinto, which was owner of a large part of the north of the island. He was also able to persuade his fellow directors to run telephone and power lines underground. Up to now only one sky scraper has been built in Arrecife, which Manrique describes as "a crime against the spirit of the island". Manrique is said to have been in New York for some time when it was being built. He promoted a traditional cubic architectural form. A house can grow; the Lanzaroteños begin with one or two rooms, when the family grows, they build new one- or two storey cubes onto it. The rooms surround a patio which incorporates a well.

Manrique's notion was to build in accordance with nature and to help extend natural forms. His aim was to preserve tradition and to realize a form of architecture which was suited to the landscape and which was suited in particular to the island's natural features. He was in direct contact with nature, working from and with it. He was also a person who was aware of his fellow beings and considers them in his work. He has brought nature out from behind the scenes, made it visible, preventing overdevelopment by supporting the construction of tourist centres. He designed a form of architecture which was conducive to a pleasant life style.

Manrique proposed the projects, planned them, saw them through, but took no commission. His work was a present to the people of Lanzarote. Manrique lived from his private commissions and his painting.

He realized his desire to live with the lava in his own house in Tahiche, which he has recently endowed to his fellow citizen. He erected the house, with its characteristic, Lanzarotean cubic form, across seven volcanic bubbles on a bluish black lava stream. Apart from the bell tower, the external architectural form of the house is not much different from the other houses (→ Fundación César Manrique). He has made a house of the Muses out of the lava bubbles, hollow chambers about five metres in diameter, which were formed as the lava solidified.

Manrique took care of nature avoiding ugly architectural forms. And it was his aim to protect Lanzarote from bad construction. He has, in part, succeeded. He has also made the architecture more uniform. The whitewashed walls, doors and windows painted green and the almost uniform cubic architectural style recur so often that it becomes almost unbearable. A red tiled roof, a beige external wall, or a door or window turning slightly blue are refreshing sights. But these are mere details, compared to his great achievements.

Manrique was the impetus behind a humane form of architecture, he set decisive accents. However, his influence was not enough, capitalist interests were pushed through; ever more barbarians were at work. The architectural style which was developed from the traditional style was being imitated and turned into kitsch.

Manrique himself spoke of "stupid, brutal speculators". After the firm of Río Tinto – where Manrique was once artistic director –

experienced economic difficulties, commercial interests grew. Market forces became the decisive factor behind new construction and the firm built indiscriminately, no longer heeding the artist's advice. They built with complete disregard for the many agreements made for many years; indeed they are still building. Manrique's name was also misused for their own purposes, although he had long since resigned from Río Tinto.

He died at the age of seventy-three years, fit and full of vitality in a accident near Arrecife on 25th September 1992 six months after the opening of his foundation, which he left during his lifetime to the population of Lanzarote.

Fundación César Manrique

16.
THE NEIGHBOURING ISLANDS

G RACIOSA is the geological continuation of Lanzarote. The two massifs are separated by a 1.5–2 km wide strait called El Río. The name of the island of Graciosa, which is 27 square metres large, means "the graceful" and was given to the island by Jean de Béthencourt. The island is shaped by its four volcanoes, the highest of which is the Pedro Barba (bearded Petrus), measuring 266 m.

A little more than 500 people still live very authentically in the villages of Caleta del Sebo and Pedro de Barba. Many of its inhabitants work on Lanzarote. Graciosa is the ideal place for divers, underwater photographers, anglers, dreamers and people in search of peace, sun and sand. The larger part of the island is covered in golden sand dunes and holds much undisturbed beauty. Graciosa is one of the most beautiful places for bathing on the Canary archipelago. By renting a bicycle or by jeep (you are driven) you can reach the Playa de las Conchas beach, which stretches for several kilometres on the other side of the island. From there you can see the next island, Montaña Clara.

There are no hotels on Graciosa; however, there is a complex of holiday apartments now. You can find simple accommodation in two pensions in Caleta del Sebo.

MONTAÑA CLARA (light mountains) is uninhabited. This dead landscape is situated two kilometres north of Graciosa. It is just one km large, with only one volcano, measuring 256 m, no beaches, hardly any vegetation. This island, which is almost entirely covered in pyroclastica, is worthless for tourism (Pyroclastica is the general name for loose volcanic waste such as tephra and tuff).

ALEGRANZA ("joy"), measuring 12 km, is the most northernly island of the Canarian archipelago. It has several volcanoes, the highest measuring 289 m. The earth is covered for the larger part in lava ash and pyroclastica. The coastline is rocky and stoney with little bays. There is an ornithological station and a the island was a former bird paradise. You can make a trip from Graciosa to Alegranza.

ROQUE DEL OESTE (ROQUE DEL INFIERNO) and ROQUE DEL ESTE are the tips of volcanoes on the sea bed, which are situated to the north west and east of Graciosa.

LOBOS was named Magi-Mani earlier, and was Béthencourt's refuge. It was certainly once a good hide-out for pirates and slave traders and owes its name to the herds of robbers who stopped here on their voyages. Lobos means wolves and the name refers to the *lobos marinos*, the seals. Most of the island is covered with pyroclastica and its highest point is 122 m. The coastline is rocky, but there are some nice bays for bathing. There is a good area for diving and snorkeling between Lobos and Fuerteventura. Every now and again it is possible to make a trip in one of the private boats – enquire at Playa Blanca harbour for the best information. One family lives on Lobos, and also run it.

SAN BORONDÓN is a dream island: uninhabited, mysterious, an island that roams around and is exempt from tourism. It is said to have surfaced and disappeared again in various places in the Atlantic. It is an island of high mountains and deep valleys, divided by wide rivers. Rivers that are non existant on the other islands and which provide the tropical fauna with water.

This island has been known by different names: *Perdida* (the lost island), *Encantada* (the enchanted island) or *Encubierta* (the undiscovered) and is included on medieval maps. According to legend, the Irish monk Saint Brendan (also Borondón) is said to have gone to sea on the back of a giant whale, in search of paradise. The Canary people changed the whale into an island which is supposed to have been spotted in different places. If one approached it, it disappeared. Scientists soberly put it down as a fata morgana.

Graciosa. Montaña Clara, Alegranza; bottom: Lobos

III
SERVICE SECTION

1. TOWNS AND SIGHTS WITH RECOMMENDED RESTAURANTS AND ACCOMMODATION, ESSENTIAL INFORMATION, AND THE FOLLOWING SPECIAL REPORTS

The following chapter, Towns and Sights, is in alphabetical order, and intended as a reference aid to discovering the island. Items include all the sights and essential information, including tips on where to eat well, and special places to stay. The essential information is for use when required. And we also tell you where you can go dancing, and when the villages hold their fiestas – the date we give is the main day of the fiesta, with actual celebrations usually beginning two weeks earlier. These village festivals have both religious and folk roots. The processions held on the main fiesta days are an experience not to be missed.

Arrecife

The capital and administrative centre of Lanzarote is the home of approx. 30,000 people. Translated, Arrecife means – rocky reef. In the town's harbour stands the largest fishing fleet of the Canary archipelago.

Banks, shops, bars and restaurants can be found on the sea promenade, the Avenida del Generalissimo Franco and in the Calle León y Castillo, which runs from the Castillo de San Gabriel into town. The nearby parallel streets also have many shops and bars.

Going towards the Charco de San Ginés, the small lake, which was formed and delicately reinforced and bridged by Manrique, one comes across the simple church Parroquia San Ginés with its square tower and colonial facade.

Continuing in this direction one reaches the harbour and the Castillo de San José. Arrecife is a town to discover oneself (see the map of the town on the back cover).

★ Castillo de San José

At César Manrique's suggestion, the fort at the harbour entrance of Puerto de Naos was restored in 1968 and turned into a museum for contemporary art. Manrique also had a restaurant built onto the Castillo. The Castillo itself is open from 11.00–21.00 hrs, the restaurant from 11.00–24.00 hrs.

★ Castillo de San Gabriel

Situated on the Isla de San Gabriel near Arrecife, the Castillo was originally a wooden fortress, which could not withhold the many attacks by pirates. It was reinforced twice. The first time was in 1572 by the Spanish fortress builder Sancho de Selín, who turned the Castillo into a stone fort. The second time was according to the plans of the Italian fortress builder Leonardo Torriani. It was reinforced in 1590, after the reinforcements of 1586 proved too flimsy, to with-hold a pirate attack by Morato Arráez. Today the Castillo houses an archeological museum. You can reach the Castillo from the sea promenade across a stone dam or a rail bridge, the so-called *Puente de las Bolas* (the ball bridge), which is the emblem of Lanzarote. Open from Monday to Friday 9.00–14.45 hrs.

★ Casa de los Arroyo

Three aspects are combined in this museum in the Avda. Gen. Franco, diagonally opposite the bridge of spheres: the architecture, archeology and art of Pancho Lasso. You will also find temporary exhibitions. Open from Monday to Friday 10.30–13.30 and 16.00–19.00 hrs.

CASTILLO DE SAN JOSÉ

The fortress was built between 1776–1779, no longer to secure the harbour de Naos for the military; there was nothing left to defend. With the construction of the Castillo, King Carlos III rather aimed to appease the lack of food. The Lanzaroteños suffered from lack of food continuously between 1703 and 1779. It was for this reason that the Spanish king tried to provide work with the *Fortaleza del Hambre* (Hunger fortress) and to make survival easier.

Claudio de Lisle had the fortress built 70 m above the harbour of Arrecife. Until 1890 the fortress was used as a powder store, afterwards it stood empty. In 1968 César Manrique suggested renovating the Castillo and fitting it out as a museum for contemporary art (Museo de Arte Contemporáneo).

An institution was founded and Manrique was made its honorary director. It was also he who took charge of the architecture and put the collection together. It was opened in 1976 with big names: Joan Miró, Pablo Picasso, Sam Francis, Antonio Tápies and many others. Manrique put together a museum which matched up to the standards of the world wide art scene. The paintings and sculpture are changed regularly. The collection cost the citizens of Lanzarote not one peseta.

At the Castillo Manrique also had a restaurant built, the ground plans of which he drew directly onto the earth with chalk – without any draft. Today one can dine there looking down at the harbour and with pleasant music playing in the background. It is even played in the toilets. Concerts are occasionally given in the upper exhibition hall. The Castillo is open from 11.00–21.00 hrs, the restaurant from 11.00–24.00 hrs, you can dine from 13.00–15.30 and after 20.00 hrs.

★ Almacén

Is situated in the Calle José Betancort, no. 33, and was once a residential house (*almacén* = store, department store). Manrique and others bought it and opened it as a arts centre in 1974. It was of course Manrique who was in charge of the conversion. Today the Almacén is owned by the municipality. There is a bar, the Pablo Ruiz Picasso restaurant, a book store and the office of the Cultural Administration. In the cellar Manrique had an old well turned into the El Aljibe gallery.

ᵞᵎ Marisquería Mesón Los Troncos

Excellent sea-food restaurant with unusual fish dishes. You will find it in Calle Agustín de la Hoz, 9 (by Puerto de Naos). Open 13.30–16.30 hrs and from 20.00 hrs. Reservations: Tel. 928 81 36 37.

🏛 Hotel Lancelot

Avenida Mancomunidad, 9, Tel. 928 80 50 99, Fax 928 80 50 39. Three stars.

🏛 Hotel-Residencia Miramar

Calle Coll, 2. Tel. 928 81 04 38. Three stars.

✚ Hospital General de Lanzarote

Carretera Arrecife – Tinajo km 1.3. Tel. 928 80 17 52 / 928 80 16 36.

⚓ Policía

Guardia Civil, Calle Apolo, 3. Tel. 928 81 18 86.

⚔ Discotecas

In the Calle José Antonio, you will find the following discotheques and music cafés: La Antiqua, La Fabrica, La Polinesia, El Volcano and El Convento.

🚗 Taxi

Tel. 928 80 31 04.

⚔ Fiesta

Fiesta de San Ginés on 25th August and Fiesta de la Virgen del Rosario on 7th October.

Arrieta

This village on the north coast should not be left out when a tour of the north is made. Not just because of the nearby sights such as Los Jameos del Agua and the Cueva de los Verdes. The north tour can be ended here with a first class meal of fish.

ᵞᵎ Restaurante Amanecer

In the main street. Open 12.00–20.30 hrs. Closed on Thursdays.

🏨 **Apartamentos**
Inquire in the main street, no. 33, or tel. 928 84 83 35.

Costa Teguise

Costa Teguise is the third largest tourist centre in Lanzarote after Puerto del Carmen and Playa Blanca. In 1977 the foundation stone for this area was laid with the construction of the worth-seeing five star hotel "Los Salinas" (Avda. Islas Canarias), which César Manrique helped to design. Further hotels, apartments, shops, bars and restaurants were built in quick succession. The well-kept 18-hole golf course is international standard.

🍴 **Mesón La Jordana**
One restaurant on the Costa Teguise that is particularly worthy of mention is the Mesón La Jordana with its elegant atmosphere, in the Calle Los Geranios. Its excellent international cuisine offers you a wide range of specialities. Lamb, rabbit and kid are recommended, as are fish and seafood. Open from 12.00–16.00 hrs and from 18.00–23.00 hrs. Closed on Sundays. Tel. 928 59 03 28.

🍴 **El Pueblo Marinero**
The Pueblo Marinero on the Avenida de Las Islas Canarias has several restaurants and cocktail bars, some with live music, and shopping facilities, including a pottery shop with an excellent selection.

🍴 **El Boulevard**
You will find various places to eat and drink in the El Boulevard de los Zocos, including a tapa bar, a Spanish pub, a pizzeria and tex mex. There is live music every evening.

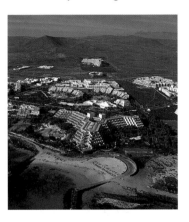

🏨 **Hotel Meliá Salinas**
One of the best hotels on Lanzarote. On the Avda. Islas Canarias. Tel. 928 59 00 40. Fax 928 59 12 32. The architecture is a point of interest, and there is a superb restaurant. Five stars.

⛵ **Surfing**
The F2 surfing school by the beach, to the right of Las Cucharas. Daily 9.30–17.00 hrs.

🤿 **Centro de Buceo**
The diving school is by the beach, next to the surfing school. Open 8.30–18.00 hrs Mon–Sat.

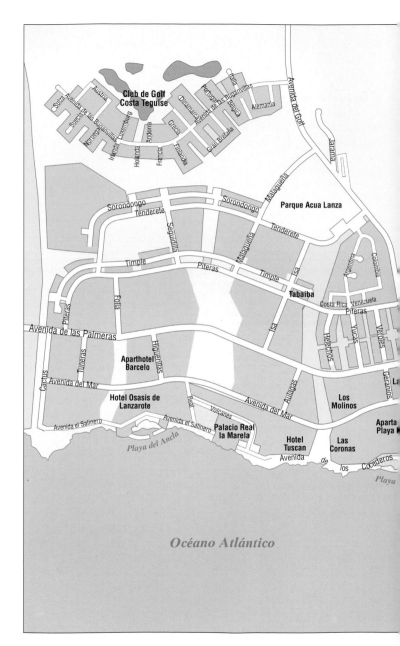

Club de Golf
Costa Teguise

Austria

Suiza

Avenida de las Buganvillas

Suecia

Noruega

Irlanda

Holanda

Luxemburgo

Andorra

Francia

Grecia

Finlandia

Dinamarca

Avenida de las Buganvillas

Portugal

Italia

Bélgica

Gran Bretaña

Alemania

Avenida del Golf

Jarama

Sorondongo

Tenderete

Sorondongo

Malagueña

Parque Acua Lanza

Tenderete

Sequndilla

Timple

Piteras

Timple

Malagueña

Isa

Tabaiba

Argentina

Colombia

Costa Rica

Venezuela

Piteras

Folia

Avenida de las Palmeras

Piteras

Isa

Helechos

Yucas

Veroles

Tuneras

Cactus

Higueritas

Aparthotel
Barcelo

Avenida del Mar

Geranios

La

Avenida del Mar

Aulagas

Los
Molinos

Avenida el Salinero

Hotel Osasis de
Lanzarote

Real

Volcanes

Avenida el Salinero

Palacio Real
la Marela

Aparta
Playa

Playa del Ancla

Hotel
Tuscan

Las
Coronas

Avenida

de

los

Cocederos

Playa

Océano Atlántico

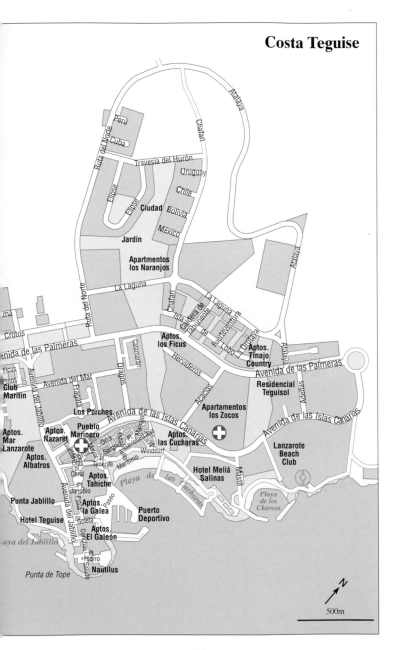

Costa Teguise

Perú
Cuba
Chafari
Atalaya
Travesía del Hurón
Uruguay
Chile
Elfise
Ciudad
Bolivia
Elfise
México
Jardín
Apartamentos los Naranjos
La Laguna
Ruta del Norte
Chafari
La Laguna de
Isla Caldera de
Calaburiente
Fuerteventura
de Lobo La
Aptos. los Ficus
Aptos. Tinajo Country
Atalaya
Crotos
Avenida de las Palmeras
Hervideros
Avenida de las Palmeras
Ficus
Pinos
Calamaran
Dragos
Acacias
Residencial Teguisol
Club Maritin
Avenida del Mar
Avenida del Jablillo
Fragata
Los Porches
Avenida de las Islas Canarias
Apartamentos los Zocos
Adelfas
Avenida de las Islas Canarias
Aptos. Mar Lanzarote
Aptos. Nazaret
Pueblo Marinero
Aptos. las Cucharas
Lanzarote Beach Club
Aptos. Albatros
Windsurf
Marítimo
Aptos. Tahiche
Playa de las Cucharas
Hotel Meliá Salinas
Mástil
Punta Jablillo
Aptos. la Galea
Puerto Deportivo
Playa de los Charcos
Hotel Teguise
Aptos. El Galeón
Avenida del Jablillo
Salado
Pl. Hierro
Nautilus
aya del Jablillo
Punta de Tope

N

500m

★ **Agua Lanza**

Agua Lanza is a water amusement park with a variety of water slides. Below the golf course. Open daily 10.00–17.00 hrs.

☑ **Golf Costa Teguise**

This well-tended 18-hole course above Costa Teguise is of international standard. Tel. 928 59 05 12. Fax 928 59 04 90.

🏃 **Discotecas**

Each hotel has its own discotheque. We recommend the Club Aguamarina in the Los Zocos. Open Son–Thurs. 20.00–2.00 hrs and Fri–Sat 20.00–4.00 hrs.

✚ **Clínica Dr. Mager**

Behind the Pueblo Marinero. Open Mon–Thurs 10.00–13.00 and 18.00–20.00 hrs, and Fri and Sat 10.00–13.00 hrs. Tel. 928 59 24 49, in urgent cases 928 51 26 11.

🚖 **Taxi**

Tel. 928 59 08 63, 928 59 00 95 und 928 59 01 60.

El Golfo

El Golfo is a crater half devoured by the sea, a crescent shape towering over the black beach and the green lagoon, whose water enters underground from the sea. And it is also a village.

★ **Charco de los Clicos**

A short footpath from the car-

park leads to the lagoon, which is rich in micro-organisms and fed underground from the sea.

★ **Los Hervideros**

Situated in the middle between the Salinas of Janubio and El Golfo. Los Hervideros is a "volcanic exhaust pipe", which leads to the sea. The erosions in the cliff are interesting and fountains of water when the seas are high.

🍴 **Restaurante Mar Azul**

The Restaurante Mar Azul just before at the end of town is excellent, being one of the best fish restaurants on the island. The specialities are: freshly caught fish (pescado fresco), red king prawns (carabineros).

🍴 **Restaurante Placido**

The oldest fish restaurant in El Golfo offers lovely surroundings to sit in. Open 12.00–21.00 hrs. Closed on Mondays.

🍴 **Restaurante Casa Torano**

This is a highly recommended fish restaurant, located just before the Restaurante Mar Azul. A fish restaurant where they serve not only fish, but also meat and paella. Ask what the day's catch is.

🏛 **El Hotelito**

The Hotelito del Golfo has five rooms, making it the smallest hotel on Lanzarote. Tel./Fax 928 17 32 72.

Top: El Golfo; bottom: Los Hervideros

El Grifo

El Grifo is the name of the 40-hectare vinyard, situated at the geographic centre of the island near Masdache.

★ Museo del Vino

The wine museum in the Bodegas El Grifo near Masdache, three kilometres from the Monumento al Campesino, is worth a visit. There are some old wine-producing tools to be seen, and a laboratory too. Guided walk through the vinyard. This is the only vintners' in the Canary Isles that also produces sparkling wine. You can buy some excellent wines here. Open daily 10.30–18.00 hrs. Admission free.

MUSEO DEL VINO

At the geographical centre of Lanzarote, near Masdache and three kilometres from the Monumento al Campesino, lie the vinyards of El Grifo. The privately owned Bodegas El Grifo is the oldest and largest vintners' still working in the Canary Isles.

A fascinating wine museum has been set up in the old buildings of the wine cellar, which has been in use since 1775, to show you the history of wine production at El Grifo. On display are old grape-presses, the wine cellar, wine-producing machines and tools, and a laboratory. There are marked paths to guide you on a half-hour walk through the 40 hectares of vinyard (wear suitable shoes!)

There is also a small bar serving the various wines available at the Bodega El Grifo. Apart from the heavy Lanzarotean wines of malvasia and muscatel grapes, there are also the light, dry white wines and a rosé, and a very presentable young red wine. The Bodegas El Grifo is the only vintners' in the Canary Isles that also produces sparkling wine. Called Malvasía Brut Nature, it is without doubt one of the finest wines produced on the archipelago.

Along the road leading to the vinyard is the Monumento al Pájaro Grifo, made by César Manrique. The El Grifo (or Grifín or Grifón) is a gryphon, a divine creature from Greek mythology that represents the four elements water, fire, air and earth. Open daily 10.30–18.00 hrs. Admission free.

Femés

This mountain village can be reached via Las Casitas from Uga, or via Las Breñas. It is situated in a wind gap, which provices a wonderful vantage point over Montaña Roja and Playa Blanca. The church was officially opened on 17th February 1733, during the mighty volcanic eruptions (1730–1736). It carries the name of the island's patron saint: Marcial del Rubicón.

¶¶ Restaurante Casa Emiliano

The Casa Emiliano is a classic local inn with good Canary Isles food and a family atmosphere. The rabbit and kid dishes can be particularly recommended. The panorama terrace affords a wonderful view across to Lobos and Fuerteventura. Open 11.30–22.30 hrs. Tel. 928 83 02 23.

¶¶ Restaurante Balcón de Femés

This restaurant serves Canary Isle and international cuisine, and here too the rabbit and kid are particularly recommended. The panorama balcony also gives you a magnificent view across to Lobos and Fuerteventura, and you can enjoy the sunset. Open daily from 10.00–23.00 hrs.

♣ Fiesta

Fiesta de San Marcial del Rubicón (the island's patron saint) on 7th July.

Guatiza

In the north of Lanzarote, at and around Guatiza and Mala, you will be amazed to see giant fields of cactus, used for the cultivation of cochineal. The cochineal beetle (coccus cacti), which originates in Mexico, provides the red dye of carmine acid, which was highly prized before the invention of aniline dyes. At the centre of the cactus fields, at the foot of the Guatiza mill, César Manrique designed a cactus garden.

★ Jardín de Cactus

This museum of cactus is well worth seeing, with 9,700 plants, 1,420 different species, mainly imported from America. Open from 10.00–18.00 hrs.

Guinate

En route from Haría to Mirador del Río via Máguez, it is worth making a detour to Guinate.

★ Mirador la Graciosa

You will come straight to the edge of the cliff coast, from which you will have a wonderful view across to Graciosa.

★ Parque Tropical

The Parque Tropical was created on terraces covering an area of 45,000 square metres. The park is home to 300 different species of bird. Open daily from 10.00–17.00 hrs. Tel. 928 83 55 00.

JARDÍN DE CACTUS

César Manrique even erected a monument to cactus. Around and at Guatiza and Mala, in the north of the island, the visitor is surprised by the gigantic cactus fields used for the cultivation of cochineal. Like the fig cactus (opuntia ficus indica), the cochineal beetle (coccus cacti) has been imported from Mexico. The cochineal beetle is a parasite on the fleshy lobes of the opuntia, but its larvae supply the red dye of carmine acid, which was once greatly coveted, before the invention of aniline dyes.

Right in the middle of this agricultural landscape, at the foot of the mill of Guatiza, the government has had a cactus garden laid out according to Manrique's ideas. In front of it is an eight-metre metal cactus statue, loosely based on the cactus pachycereus grandis. Turning this eroded place with its bizarrely weathered monoliths into a museum of cacti in this way was typical of César Manrique's way of working.

Farmers had dug this pit by hand around 1850. They had transported the loose volcanic rock to their fields by donkey-cart to protect the fields from drying out. The remaining monoliths could not be removed as the rock was too hard – in those days there were no machines.

Today, 1,420 species grow here, with a total of 9,700 plants. Most of the cactus species come from America, a few come from Madagascar and the Canary Isles. Some of them are fully grown at two to three centimetres, while others such as the caneja gigantea attain heights of twenty-five metres. The most remarkable specimen on show is the euphorbia handiensis, which grows exclusively on Fuerteventura. Open from 10.00–18.00 hrs.

Haría

Situated in the valley of a thousand palms, this village has an oriental feel to it. The North African architecture, the cubic white houses and the numerous palm trees give this impression. The palm which has taken to this place most is the golden fruit palm; its fruit is not edible however. Haría often gives the impression of being a ghost town, although almost 3,000 people live there. If one approaches Teguise from Los Valles, there is a wonderful view of the village from the pass road at the Mirador del Haría. In the centre of the village one can enjoy the shadow and peace under the Laurels and acacias.

★ Museo de Miniaturas

Next to the Restaurante El Cortijo, you will find a museum of miniatures, with the smallest works of art in the world. Open daily 10.00–18.00 hrs.

🍴 Restaurante El Cortijo

If you approach Haría from Teguise, on the edge of town you will find an old farmhouse on the left. This has been converted into a restaurant and provides excellent Canarian and international cuisine. Open from 11.00–22.00 hrs.

🍴 Restaurante Casa'l Cura

This is a typical Canary Isles inn, lying on the road out of town in the direction of Máguez, in Calle Nueva, 1. Among the specialities: roast lamb and goatmeat. Open daily 12.00–17.00 hrs.

🏃 Fiesta

Fiesta de San Juan am 24th June and Fiesta de Santa Rosa 30th August.

La Caleta

A small fishing village, 16 km from Mozaga and 8 km north of Teguise. This is home to one of the most beautiful beaches in Lanzarote, the Playa de Famara. In contrast to others, this beach has a rough sea climate. Very strong currents! Swimming can be highly dangerous to life and limb. The coast suitable for surfing and wave riding. It is worth taking a walk through the actual village.

⚍ Restaurante El Risco

Excellent fish restaurant in the town on the coast. Ask for the catch of the day. Open daily 12.00–21.30 hrs.

La Geria

The farmers on Lanzarote painstakingly cultivate their vinyards right up to the peaks of the volcanoes, creating a landscape architecture that is unique. If you would like to taste this excellent country wine far away from the tourist crowds, we recommend the relaxing atmosphere of Bodega El Chupadero.

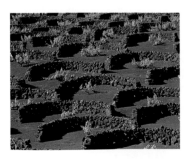

⚍ Bodega El Chupadero

If you drive out 4 km from Uga in the direction of Teguise, you will come to a chapel. 200 m further along on the right side, you will see the signpost indicating the turn-off to the bodega. It is at present still only known to insiders. To go with the wine, there are little delicacies to eat. 10.00–20.00 hrs.

La Santa

The fishing village is in the north of Lanzarote, just after Tinajo. 7 kilometres north of La Santa is one of the best-equipped sporting complexes in Europe, where top world-famous sports personalities train.

⚍ Restaurantes

There are a variety of very good fish restaurants in the town of La Santa.

🏛 Albergue juvenil

The only youth hostel on Lanzarote is under construction in La Santa, due to open its doors from 1999.

🏛 Club La Santa

Hotel complex to the north of La Santa, with one of the best-equipped sports facilities in Europe. You can practise any of over twentyfive different sports disciplines here. There are also various restaurants, bars, a supermarket, a shopping centre and plenty of entertainment for children. Tel. 928 84 01 00. Fax 928 84 00 50.

LA GERIA

Around Geria lies Lanzarote's wine-producing region, which is a sight worth seeing in itself. From Uga to San Bartolomé, nature has covered the earth with a broad strip of pyroclastic material from the volcanoes, the black picón. Deep circular funnels have been dug out so that the vines can reach the fertile soil with their roots. These earthworks go back to the 18th century, when the malvasia grape was introduced from Crete. The winegrowers built little walls of volcanic stone round the funnels, known as *zocos*, to protect the vines from the drying wind. The entire vineyard region covers around 3,000 hectare. With its spicy, dry bouquet, the amber-coloured malvasia with wine is one of the best wines on the Canary archipelago. It thrives in ideal conditions of low rainfall, strong sun and fertile volcanic oil.

Los Valles

The valleys. They are situated 5 km from Teguise on the way to Haría. Interesting landscape. The terraced fields are impressive as is the view towards the south when one reaches the end of the valley. In 1730, Santa Catalina was buried in a volcanic eruption, and 42 of its inhabitants fled to Los Valles de Santa Catalina.

★ Casa de los Peraza

The Casa de los Peraza, which today belongs to the office of the mayor of Teguise, was built in the first half of the 15th century. There are plans to set up an ethnographic museum in the renovated buildings.

⅋ Restaurante Mirador del Valle

The Mirador del Valle is a restaurant with a wonderful view across Los Valles. We recommend both the Canary Isles food and the international cuisine. Open daily 11.00–22.00 hrs.

Mácher

Situated between Uga and Tías. Village passed on the way to elsewhere. Turning for Puerto del Carmen and, by crossing La Asomada, to the wine growing region.

⅋ Restaurante El Pozo

Excellent restaurant specialising in fine Italian and international cuisine. Quality wines are served. The restaurant is in Mácher, on the main road between Tías and Uga, on the left as you come from Uga. Open 18.30–23.30 hrs, closed on Mondays. Tel. 928 51 24 54 / 928 51 26 77.

⩩ Multi-Center-Mácher

Half-way along the main road between Mácher and Puerto del Carmen there is a shopping and garden centre that is well worth a visit (turn off at Restaurante La Finca). The merchandise includes Canary Isles pottery, folk articles, quality souvenirs, blankets and much more. If you have forgotten to bring something, or are looking for a present, this is the place to come.

The garden centre, which was designed by an English landscape designer, is a shopping experience, with a great variety of plants. Your purchase will be packed for travelling. Mon-Fri 9.00–19.30 hrs, Sat 9.00–13.00 hrs. Tel. 928 51 35 51.

Mala

The village is situated in the north east of the island between Guatiza and Arrieta and is surrounded by cactus plantations, where the cochineal beetle is bred.

Mancha Blanca

Situated between the Montañas del Fuego and Tinajo, the area was the victim of the last volcanic eruptions in 1824. The Ermita de los Dolores is worth seeing. The church dates from the 18th century and is the home of the volcanic saint: Nuestra Señora de los Volcanes. According to legend Dolores diverted the burning stream of lava, flowing from Volcano Quemada, with her hand and saved the farmers' houses and fields from obliteration.

🏃 Fiesta

Fiesta de Nuestra Señora de los Volcanes on 15th September.

During the fiesta there is also a craft fair which is well worth seeing. The fiesta itself is one of the most beautiful on the island.

Masdache

Situated in the wine growing region between La Geria and Mozaga. The town is surrounded by unique scenery, shaped like a sea of ice that is melting and breaking up, and whose crust has collapsed in some places, with the ice-floes pushed up on top of one another. Only these ice-floes are covered in green lichen.

Mozaga

The Fertililty Monument stands here in the geographical centre of Lanzarote.

🍴 Casa del Campesino

Typical Canarian cuisine, with specialities that are well worth trying. Open daily from 12.30–16.00 hrs.

Nazaret

The town is located between Teguise and Tahiche, and has a modern part with villas. The attraction for holiday-makers is an unusual restaurant, the Lagomar.

🍴 Café-Restaurante Lagomar

Lagomar, at the foot of the Volcán de Nazaret, is a fascinating place where nature and art join hands. This is a real must. The restaurant serves first-class Mediterranean cuisine. The café is open 12.00–23.00 hrs, the restaurant 13.00–16.00 hrs and 20.00–23.00 hrs. Closed on Sunday evenings and Mondays. Tel. 928 84 56 65.

CASA MUSEO Y MONUMENTO AL CAMPESINO

The monument to the hard working and ingenious farmers bears the name: *Fecundidad al Campesino Lanzaroteño* (Fertility for the Lanzarotean Farmers) and stands shortly before Mozaga in the geographical centre of the island. The sculpture, which is 15 m high was designed by Manrique and realized by J. Soto in 1968. It is composed of former water tanks, wrecked fishing boats and cutters and depicts the farmer with his cattle.

The Farmer's House *(Casa Museo al Campesino)* stands next to it; it is a renovated and extended farmstead with which Manrique probably wanted to make a monument to the architecture of the island. A museum, shop and restaurant, serving typical Canary dishes, form a part of this farmstead. It is well worth trying Canary specialities here.

Orzola

The name Orzola probably originates from "oursolle", the old description for orchilla, the lichen used for dye. Orzola, the most northerly village in Lanzarote, situated nine kilometres from Los Jameos del Agua, is a dreamy place which is well worth visiting. There are beautiful beaches, covered in a fine layer of Muschelkalk on the way to Orzola from Jameos del Agua. The Playa de la Cantería is to the west of Orzola. It is dangerous to swim at the end of the cove in Orzola, the current is very strong and it even sometimes causes larger boats trouble.

🍴 Restaurante Punta Fariones

The Punta Fariones restaurant, on the left-hand side just before the harbour, is well worth a visit, serving you freshly cought fish and excellent seafood. Open daily from 11.00 – 24.00 hrs.

🚤 Guacimara

If you want to do some deep-sea angling or take a boat trip to the outlying islands, got to the Restaurante Punta Fariones and ask for David, who will take you wherever you wish to go in his boat, the Guacimara (up to 25 persons). Tel. 928 84 25 58.

🚤 Graciosa

You can take a launch across to Graciosa.

Orzola – Caleta del Sebo
10.00, 12.00, 17.00 hrs
(and at 18.30 hrs in summer)
Caleta del Sebo – Orzola
8.00, 11.00, 16.00 hrs
(and at 18.00 hrs in summer)

🏛 Alojamiento en Graciosa

Pension Enriqueta: Rooms, some with shower and toilet. Tel. 928 84 20 51.

Pension Girasol Playa: Simple rooms. Tel. 928 84 21 18.

Apartamentos Romero: Tel. 928 84 20 55.

124

Playa Blanca

Once a sleepy little fishing village, this is now gradually developing into a major tourist resort. The promenade with its little sandy beach is an attraction in Playa Blanca.

★ Playas de Papagayo

About four kilometres from the town of Playa Blanca, there is a series of sandy beaches around the Punta de Papagayo. The beaches are part of the Los Ajaches region, which has been declared a nature benchmark, or natural monument. There is an admission fee for driving into this region.

★ Castillo de las Coloradas

Stands on the Punta del Águila one kilometre east of Playa Blanca and dates from the 18th century. From here one can gain a wonderful view right across the sea. This is the point from which "attackers" were once spotted. One can see across the Papagayo beaches to Playa Blanca and across to the next island, Fuerteventura. The Castillo itself is locked.

⁞⁞ Restaurante Brisa Marina

The Brisa Marina restaurant is in the middle of the promenade that forms part of the old part of Playa Blanca. Freshly caught fish and fresh seafood daily. Canarian and international cuisine.

⁞⁞ Restaurante Almacén de la Sal

The Almacén de la Sal restaurant has been created in a century-old salt storehouse right next to the beach, and serves exquisite Basque and international cuisine, in an interior that is an experience. Enjoy the live music in the evenings. Open daily from 10.00–24.00 hrs.

⁞⁞ Casa Brigida

On the access road to Playa Blanca, 100 metres before the roundabout on the left-hand side. Excellent Canarian cuisine. Brigida also rents rooms. Closed on Mondays.

⁞⁞ Restaurante Romantica

One of the best restaurants in Lanzarote. We particularly recommend the lamb dishes, and the fresh meat dishes prepared on the charcoal barbecue. Fine wines are served. Calle Limones, 6, on the first floor above the Pizzería Borsalino. Open 12.00–16.00 and 18.30–24.00 hrs. Closed on Thursdays. Tel. 928 51 71 66.

⁞⁞ Pizzería Borsalino

If you like a well-made pizza or fresh, home-made pasta, the Pizzería Borsalino is the place for you. International cuisine is also served. In the Calle Limones, 6. Open 10.00–23.00 hrs. Closed on Sundays. Tel. 928 51 71 68.

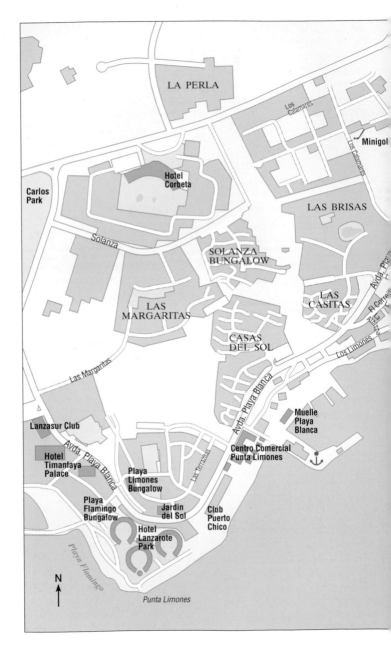

LA PERLA

Los Catamares

Minigol

Hotel
Corbeta

Carlos
Park

LAS BRISAS

Solanza

SOLANZA
BUNGALOW

LAS
CASITAS

LAS
MARGARITAS

El Cerrillo

Avda. Playa

Adisba

CASAS
DEL SOL

Los Limones

Las Margaritas

Avda. Playa Blanca

Muelle
Playa
Blanca

Lanzasur Club

Avda. Playa Blanca

Hotel
Timanfaya
Palace

Playa
Limones
Bungalow

Las Terrazas

Centro Comercial
Punta Limones

Playa
Flamingo
Bungalow

Jardin
del Sol

Club
Puerto
Chico

Hotel
Lanzarote
Park

Playa Flamingo

N

Punta Limones

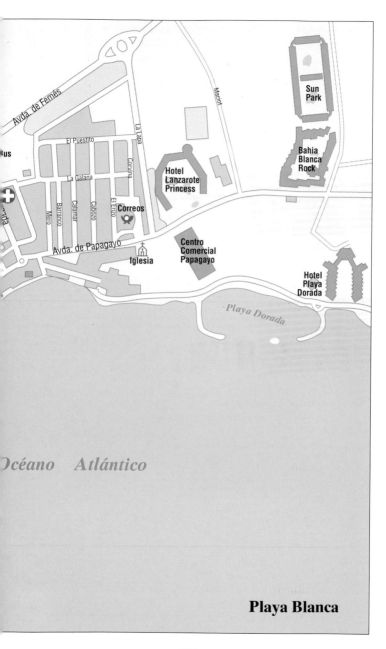

Avda. de Femés

El Puestito

La Lapa

La Galana

Corvina

Hotel
Lanzarote
Princess

Barranco

Calamar

Cabozo

El Erizo

Mero

Correos

Avda. de Papagayo

Iglesia

Centro
Comercial
Papagayo

Marlot

Sun
Park

Bahia
Blanca
Rock

Hotel
Playa
Dorada

Playa Dorada

Océano   Atlántico

Playa Blanca

Restaurante Mar de Plata

The restaurant terrace is a good place to sit, admiring the view across to Fuerteventura. Good international food. There is live music in the evening, and if you don't want to eat, you can try one of the cocktails. Open daily 9.00–24.00 hrs. Tel. 928 51 77 45.

Restaurante El Mandarin

In the Centro Comercial Papagayos, below the Hotel Princess, you will find an excellent Chinese restaurant. Open daily 12.30–15.30 and 19.30–23.30 hrs. Closed on Monday mornings and on Saturday mornings. Tel. 928 51 76 31.

Hotel Lanzarote Park

A quality hotel directly on the sea-front. Tel. 928 51 70 48. Fax 928 51 73 48. Three stars.

Hotel Timanfaya Palace

An exclusive hotel on the sea-front. Tel. 928 51 76 76. Fax 928 51 70 35. Four stars.

Hotel Playa Dorada

On the well-tended Playa Dorada. Tel. 928 51 71 20, Fax 928 51 74 32. Four stars.

Centro de Buceo

The Las Toninas diving centre is in the Hotel Playa Flamingo. Open daily, 9.30–18.00 hrs in summer, 10.00–18.00 hrs in winter. Tel. 928 51 73 00. Fax 928 51 76 42.

Aquascope

On the harbour of Playa Blanca. You can watch the underwater world from the aquascope. Departures daily 10.00–20.00 hrs. Tel. 928 64 74 67.

Marea Errota

Spend the whole day on the two-masted wooden schooner 24 metres in length, with full board. The "pirate ship" Marea Errota is berthed in the Playa Blanca harbour. Inquire at your hotel or apartment block reception for further information. Tel. 928 51 76 33. Fax 928 51 75 14.

Discotecas

Most hotels have their own discotheques. On the whole, though, night life in Playa Blanca is still a bit sparse. In the Centro Comercial Yaiza, in the first centre on the left as you drive in, you will find the Aquarius night bar and the Mururoa discotheque, and in the Centro Comercial Punta Limones on the harbour, there are a number of pubs with live music and karaoke.

PLAYAS DE PAPAGAYO

About four kilometres from the town of Playa Blanca, there is a sequence of sandy bays around the Punta de Papagayo, the southernmost tip of Lanzarote.

The beaches begin at the Punta del Águila, where the Castillo de las Coloradas stands. The first is Playa de las Coloradas, which is rather stony, with black sand. A few hills and cliffs further on, the light-sanded and most beautiful beaches on Lanzarote begin, each sloping down gently into crystal-clear waters: Playa Mujeres, Playa del Pozo, up to the semicircular bay where the remains of the former village of El Papagayo can still be seen.

The Papagayo beaches are part of a 3009.5-hectare region called Los Ajaches, which in 1994 was declared a natural monument and bird protection zone. This is also home to San Marcial del Rubicón, the ruins of a Norman town dating back to 1402, which Jean de Béthencourt (1359–1426) had built. Access to this protected area is by a road blocked by a barrier at the old lime-kiln. There is a charge for driving into the area by car. The road then continues on to a number of car-parks, from which the beaches can be reached on foot. There is a camp-site at the Playa Puerto Muela.

🚢 Buganvilla Ferry
(Líneas Fred Olsen)
The ferry to Fuerteventura

We recommend Líneas Fred Olsen. The comfortable ferry has a large cafeteria, a MINI-MARKET with fantastically low prices, and a crèche.
Departures:
From Fuerteventura (Corralejo)
9.00. 11.00, 17.00, 19.00 hrs.
From Lanzarote (Playa Blanca)
8.00, 10.00, 14.00, 18.00 hrs.

🚢 Volcán de Tindaya
(Líneas Naviera Armas)
Departures:
From Fuerteventura (Corralejo)
8.00, 10.00, 14.00, 18.00 hrs.
From Lanzarote (Playa Blanca),
9.00, 11.00, 17.00, 19.00 hrs.

🚢 Lobos
The launch Poseidon departs for Lobos at 10.15 hrs. The return trip is as agreed.

✚ Clínica Dr. Mager
C/C Yaiza, Avda. de la Llegada, next to the bus-stop. Tel. 928 51 79 38.

🚗 Taxi
Tel. 928 51 71 36, 928 51 72 51.

🏃 Fiesta
Fiesta de Nuestra Señora del Carmen 16th July.

Playa Quemada
Playa Quemada is still an authentic village with it's own black beach, which will be developed turistically in the future.

Puerto Calero
Between Puerto del Carmen and Playa Quemada lies one of the finest yachting marinas in the Canary Isles. It is well worth driving down to Puerto Calero, and not only because of the yachts. There are plenty of other things to see and do there.

🍴 Restaurante
La Pappardella
Excellent Italian restaurant, run by Italians. Open 11.00–24.00 hrs throughout the week. Tel. 928 51 29 11.

🚢 Catlanza
This company offers a wide variety of watersports. You can hire various types of boat, or book an excursion on the 14-metre-long and 8-metre-wide catamaran. This leaves daily at 10.30 hrs to sail to the Papagayo beaches, where you can swim, dive and jet-ski for hours, and be served food and drink. Open 9.30–20.00 hrs. Tel. 928 51 30 22. Fax 928 51 10 01.

🚢 Submarine Safaris
Have you ever been in a submarine? The air-conditioned submarine belonging to Submarine Safaris is completely safe, and will take you down as far as 30 metres to discover Lanzarote's fascinating underwater

world. Open 9.00–19.00 hrs. Tel.
928 51 28 98. Fax 928 51 29 06.

Puerto del Carmen

Puerto del Carmen is the
main tourist resort on Lanzarote.
Between the old part of this
former fishing village and the
airport is a 12-kilometre sandy
beach, along which stretches
the international holiday centre,
from the Playa Blanca beach via
Playa de los Pocillos to Matagorda. With a wide range of facilities available, there is no lack
of entertainment.

⦚ Restaurante La Fontaine

Superb! Thomas Fox is one of
the best chefs on the island:
house-marinaded "graved" salmon on potato cakes, filet of
gallo on Lanzarote lentils, meat
from the volcanic stone barbecue … The restaurant is in the
old part of town, Calle Teide
no. 9, the street higher up and
parallel to the old harbour.
18.30–23.00 hrs. Closed on
Tuesdays. Reservations: Tel.
928 51 42 51.

⦚ Restaurante El Tomate

El Tomate is a gourmet restaurant in the Calle Jameos. The
menu provides a balanced range
of German and international cuisine, the helpings are enormous.
Coloured pens and paper pads
are provided for children. Open

Puerto del Carmen

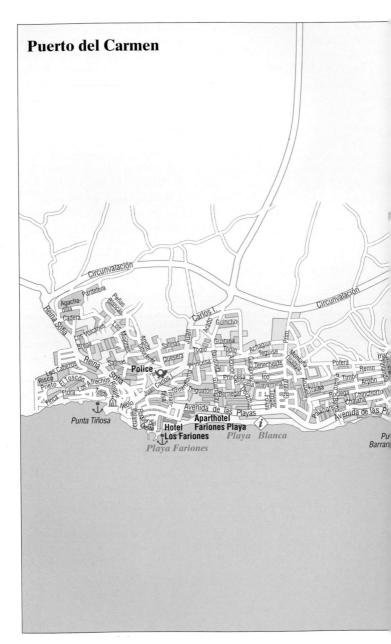

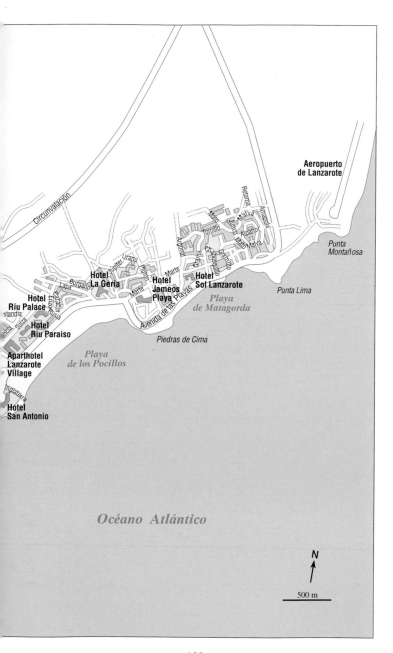

Aeropuerto
de Lanzarote

Punta
Montañosa

Retama
Maiva
Salvia
Albahor
Malva

Mato
Tomillo
Laurel
Crespino
Cremillo

Argona
Circunvalación

Hotel
La Geria

Júpiter
Urano
Plutón

Hotel
Jameos
Playa

Hotel
Sol Lanzarote

Punta Lima

Marte

Burgaño

Lapa

Saturno
Rusia

Hotel
Riu Palace

slandia

Marte

Avenida de las Playas

Playa
de Matagorda

Hotel
Riu Paraiso

Piedras de Cima

Aparthotel
Lanzarote
Víllage

Playa
de los Pocillos

Inglaterra

Hotel
San Antonio

Océano Atlántico

N

500 m

133

from 19.00 – 22.00 hrs except on Sundays. Please make a reservation. Tel. 928 51 19 85.

⏸ Pizzería Itálica

At the Pizzería Itálica they will not only offer you a wide variety of delicious pasta dishes, but also a pizza that is second to none, straight from the charcoal oven. You will find the Pizzería Itálica in the first row of buildings opposite the Los Pocillos beach, in the centre of Jameos Playa, 66. The Pizzería is open from 10.00. Tel. 928 51 16 68.

⏸ Restaurante Escuela

The Restaurante Escuela El Fondeadero on the Puerto del Carmen harbour is one of the finest eateries on Lanzarote. Open 13.30 – 15.30 hrs (apart from Monday) and 19.00 – 23.00 hrs. Closed on Thursdays. 4 forks.

⏸ El Bodegón

If you love tapas, Spanish ham and cheese, bread-rolls with all kinds of fillings, and good wine, this is the place for you. At the harbour. Entrance in Calle Ntra. Sra. del Carmen, 6. Open daily from 11.30 – 24.00 hrs. Tel. 928 51 52 65.

🏛 Apartamentos Sanos

The Sanos apartment building is situated right on the coast at Puerto del Carmen. All the apartments have a spacious livingroom and a balcony facing the sea and the sun. The furnishings are modern, and accommodation is for 2 – 6 people in each case. Tel. 928 51 35 54.

🏛 Hotel Los Fariones

At the Playa Blanca, Tel. 928 51 01 75. Four stars.

⚓ Barakuda Club

Modern equipment and 20 years of experience! Learn to dive in courses lasting 6/8 days. Individual diving trips also available! The office is in the Hotel La Geria. Mon 14.00 – 14.20 hrs and 16.30 – 17.00 hrs, Tues–Sat 9.00 – 9.20 hrs and 11.30 – 12.00 hrs. Tel. 928 51 27 65 or 608 64 72 81.

🚤 Aquascope

The aquascope is safe and air-conditioned, for you to discover the underwater world for yourself. There is a round trip half-hourly throughout the day from 10.00 hrs. Tickets can be bought at the harbour. Tel. 928 51 44 81.

🚤 Blue Delfin

Fancy a trip to Fuerteventura and Lobos? The catamaran has 32 underwater windows, and offers a 9-hour excursion with all food and refreshments, every day except Thursdays and Fridays. Tickets can be bought at the harbour. Tel./Fax 928 51 23 23.

★ Casino de Lanzarote

On the Avenida de las Playas, 12. Open daily 10.00 – 4.00 hrs. Gambling machines from 11.00

hrs. Passports or ID cards have to be shown on admission. No admittance for juveniles under 18 years. Cafeteria – restaurants – cabaret. Tel. 928 51 50 00.

🐎 Rancho Texas
The riding centre is in Cortijo de los Casalones, the quietest part of Puerto del Carmen. The options include rides for the completely inexperienced, and treks lasting all day or several hours down to the beach. There are ponies for the children. In the evenings there are country and western parties. To join in, inquire at a travel agent's or from your tour operator. Open daily 10.00–14.00 and 17.00–20.00 hrs in summer, 10.00–14.00 and 16.00–19.00 hrs in winter. Tel. 928 17 32 47. Fax 928 17 32 48.

🕺 Discotecas
There are several discotheques for you to choose from – for example, Tiffany's Hard Rock Café and Dreams. They open from 21.30 hrs on.

✚ Clínica Dr. Mager
Avda. de las Playas, 37. Tel. 928 51 26 11. Open all day.

🚕 Taxi
Tel. 928 51 36 34, 928 51 11 36, 928 51 36 38, 928 51 36 35.

🕺 Fiesta
Fiesta de Nuestra Señora del Carmen 16th July.

Punta de Mujeres
Punta de Mujeres, situated between Jameos del Agua and Arrieta, is a small fishing hamlet, which is still idyllic today.

★ Cueva de Los Verdes
The Cueva de los Verdes (Green Cave) is in the north of Lanzarote, to the south-east of Monte Corona. Part of a subterranean system seven kilometres in length, it is one of the most interesting volcanic phenomena on the island next to Los Jameos del Agua. The caves and passages have been turned into a two-kilometre circular walk for tourists – with a profound hole at the end, as it seems. Open daily from 10.00–18.00 hrs. With guided tours on the hour and every half-hour.

★ Los Jameos del Agua
Situated 250 metres from the north-eastern coast. Los Jameos del Agua was made (as was Cueva de los Verdes) by a prehistoric eruption of Monte Corona. César Manrique applied his unerring taste to the caves and gardens of Los Jameos del Agua, creating a restaurant, a night club, some little bars and a concert cave with wonderful architecture and acoustics. Los Jameos del Agua is open daily from 9.30–19.00 hrs. Additionally open from 19.00–03.00 hrs on Tuesday, Friday and Saturday, which are dance nights.

CUEVA DE LOS VERDES

To the north of Punta de Mujeres, and south east of the Monte Corona, lies the Cueva de los Verdes. The Cueva de los Verdes (Green Cave) is part of a 7 km long subterranean system and, along with Los Jameos del Agua it is one of the most interesting volcanic manifestations on the island.

The tunnel-like caves were created by a pre-historic eruption of Volcano Corona. A broad stream of lava swirled towards the east coast, but it first cooled quickly on the surface and became hard. Underneath, the lava that was still hot streamed on. By melting away old basaltic rocks, the lava eroded and flowed out. Hollow chambers were able to form. Several galleries lie above each other.

In the 17th century the Lanzaroteños used these galleries to hide from slave traders and pirates. A path around the caves and corridors, which is about 2 km long has been made for tourists. Jesús Soto provided a form of lighting which has a theatrical effect. A corresponding, often sacral sort of music is played to complete the atmosphere; it seems to emerge from every stone. The acoustics are marvelous.

The cave walls, with their lava drip stone or "stone drawings" sometimes give the impression of drawings or paintings. One corridor becomes a hall which is actually used for concert performances and can hold 100 visitors. At the end of the round trip: a profound hole. Or so it seems. But find out for yourself.

From the south you reach the Cueva de los Verdes via Arrieta or via Haría and Yé. Los Jameos del Agua are only two kilometres away; they belong to the same system of caves. The Cueva de los Verdes is open from 10.00–18.00 hrs. There are tours on the hour and every half hour

LOS JAMEOS DEL AGUA

The Los Jameos del Agua, 250 m from the north east coast, were created, like Cueva de los Verdes during a prehistoric eruption of the Monte Corona. It is part of the same system of caves and cavities which has a series of cave entrances and broken cave roofs. If one climbs down into the first "bubble", which is open at the top, the artificially laid tropical flora is at once impressive. This is immediately recognisable as the work of César Manrique.

A natural lagoon, a saltwater lake, which is connected to the sea underground, gave the grotto its name. A hole in the cave roof, which was presumably caused by a gas explosion – the stopper lies intact on the ceiling of the cave very close by – allows rays of sun through, which make the lake shimmer a dark turquoise, sometimes bluish black, sometimes steel blue. Little white, blind crabs live on the ground. These are rare shellfish, about 3 cm in length, albino crabs (Munidopsis polimorpha), designed to live deep in the sea, about 1,000 metres down. No certain explanation has been given for its appearance in Los Jameos del Agua.

Jesús Soto and Luis Morales, both experienced architects, put César Manrique's ideas into practice. It was due to their collaboration with Manrique that a restaurant, night club, small bars and a concert cave were created. They all show a wonderful flair for architecture and have marvelous acoustics. Concerts and ballet are occasionally staged here. It is well worth experiencing a performance in the concert cave.

If one follows the zig zag staircase up, one comes to a kind of walk along the battlements, which leads along the edges of the caves. At this point there is also a row of flat buildings which are destined to become a Parador Nacional (Paradores Nacionales are hotels run by the Ministry for Tourism). A museum for volcaneology has been created. Los Jameos del Agua is open daily from 9.30–19.00 hrs. On Tuesday, Friday and Saturday it is open from 19.00–03.00 hrs in addition, when there is dancing. Access is via Arrieta or from the Cueva de los Verdes.

Salinas de Janubio

In the west of Yaiza, you will find the Salinas de Janubio, the last remaining major saltworks still in use. Sea water is pumped up from Janubio, a natural lagoon, into an artificial basin, which is slightly higher, and where it stays until the salt content has risen to 22°. It is at this point that it is actually fed into the saltworks themselves. When the sticky substance has crystallized into salt, salt workers rake it up for final drying.

San Bartolomé

The village is situated in what is almost the geographical centre of the island and forms a traffic junction. It is the centre of agriculture. 4,700 people live here. San Bartolomé is also the home of Lanzarote's best known folklore group. There is a public library here and a beautifully laid out village square with the church of Parroquia de San Bartolomé at one end.

★ Go-Karting

For go-carting fans, there is an interesting track at the crossroads to Güime, between Arrecife and San Bartolomé. Children's go-carts are also available. Open 10.00–20.00 hrs.

Bar El Cruce

A wide variety of tapas. Open daily 9.00–24.00 hrs.

Fiesta

Fiesta de San Bartolomé 24th August.

Tahiche

The attraction for holidaymakers in this little town is on the road to San Bartolomé: the house where César Manrique lived until 1987 – an example of his idea of architecture and now a museum and foundation.

★ Fundación César Manrique

In 1992 César Manrique, Lanzarote's most famous artist, donated his private house in Tahiche to the public, turning it into a foundation and a museum. He had had it built over five volcanic bubbles in 1968, and lived in it himself until 1987. On display are Manrique's works: oil paintings, drawings, sketches, sculptures, ceramics, photographs and plans. The Fundación César Manrique is open Mon–Sat 10.00–18.00 hrs and Thurs 10.00–15.00 hrs from 1.11. to 30.6., and 10.00–19.00 hrs every day from 1.7. to 31.10. There is integrated a café and a bookshop.

FUNDACIÓN CÉSAR MANRIQUE

In his unpublished New York diary, César Manrique wrote in 1966 of his homesickness for Lanzarote. At the time he was still undecided as to where to set up his permanent studio. His desire to live with the lava was put into action two years later in his own house which he had built in Taro de Tahíche, and which he lived in until 1987. He donated it to his fellow citizens as a foundation in 1992.

Above five volcanic bubbles, on a blue-black lava flow, he built an architectural masterpiece in Lanzarotean cubic form. He cleverly integrated the caverns into the basic outline of the living area of 1500 square metres. The cellar-deep volcanic bubbles, connected by tunnels, became temples to the muse, each in its own different colour.

This palazzo is an impressive example of Manrique's idea of landscape-related architecture. A fig-tree which had already taken root previously grows up from the red volcanic bubble into the living-room above, now an exhibition room in which Manrique's private collection is displayed.

On show are works by Manrique: oil paintings, drawings, sketches, sculptures, ceramics, photographs and plans both of works actually carried out and works never produced.

For Manrique, who was seventy-three at the inauguration in March 1992, it was a dream come true. He regarded the foundation as the reward of his life's work.

The Fundación César Manrique is open Mon–Sat 10.00–18.00 hrs and Thurs 10.00–15.00 hrs from 1.11. to 30.6., and 10.00–19.00 hrs every day from 1.7. to 31.10. There is integrated a café and a book-shop.

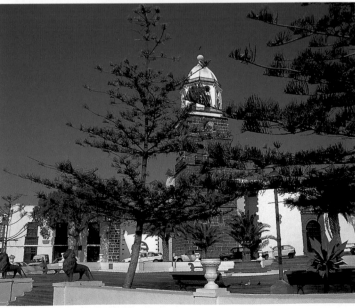

Top: Fundación César Manrique; bottom: Teguise

Teguise

Teguise, Lanzarote's most beautiful town stands beneath the Guanapays (452 m), on which the Genoan Lanzarotto Malocello had the Castillo Santa Bárbara built in the 14th century. Teguise was once the island's capital and a diocesan town. Maciot de Béthencourt had founded the town in the 15th century and had it laid out in its chess-board formation.

The interesting wooden doors and windows are rich in carving, some of the balconies are typical of the Canaries; each one has a different kind of ornamentation. The town is situated a little distance from the sea due to the numerous pirate attacks. From here one can see far into the land in an easterly direction, but Teguise was protected in the north by the precipitous coast. Nevertheless, the *Callejon de la Sangre* (the lane of blood) is a memorial to the attack by the pirate Morato Arráez in 1586 which ended in a bloody massacre.

The market place is surrounded by Teguise's most beautiful buildings: the church of Parroquia San Miguel (1680), which has a famous madonna figure; the Palacio Spinola, named after the Genoan merchant Vicente Spinola, today it is a museum well worth visiting. Two monasteries make up the townscape – the Franciscan monastery of San Francisco de Miraflores, built in the 16th century and the Santa Domingo monastery, built in the 18th century.

This century also saw the birth of the writer José Clavijo y Fajarde, probably Teguise's best known citizen. Clavijo was director of theatre at the court of Carlos III of Spain. In Madrid he seduced the milliner Lisette Caron, the sister of Pierre Augustin Caron de Beaumarchais, who was at that time living in Paris. He endeavoured to blackmail Clavijo into promising marriage to his not-so young sister; sadly his attempts were in vain. Beaumarchais eternalised the episode in his play "Eugénie". Johann Wolfgang Goethe made use of the material as a model for his tragedy "Clavigo".

Teguise is also famous for its *timple*, which is made here and is amongst one of the most frequently played string instruments on the Canary archipelago. It was invented in the 19th century by Mr John Timple. It is rather like the ukelele, the most important difference being that the *timple's* bass string is in the middle.

A market is held in Teguise on Sundays. Folklore groups sometimes perform. Artists sell pictures. There is also jewellery and ceramics for sale. Gypsies sell embroidery. The Lanzaroteños offer goat's cheese, fruit, vegetables and fish for sale. There are snack stalls, selling drinks and delicious bites to eat.

★ Palacio Spinola

The Casa Museo Palacio Spinola is today the most important and best preserved residence in Teguise, housing a museum. Open 10.00–17.00 hrs, Sat and Son until 16.00 hrs.

★ Castillo de Santa Bárbara

The Castillo de Santa Bárbara on the Guanapay volcano today houses the Canary Isles Museum of Emigrants. Open 10.00–17.00 hrs, and until 16.00 hrs Sat and Sun.

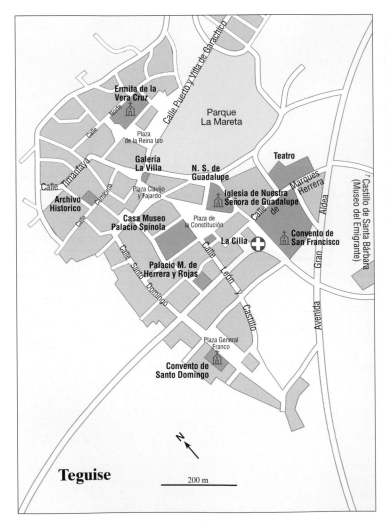

CASTILLO DE SANTA BÁRBARA

The Castillo de Santa Bárbara, on the Guanapay volcano in the eastern part of Teguise, was built by Sancho de Herrera at the beginning of the 16th century, and extended for the first time in 1551. In 1558, it was converted and reinforced by master fort builder Leonardo Torriani, who was in the service of King Felipe II. In time of war, Spain's nobles withdrew to the Castillo.

In 1998, the Teguise town council's Restauration Office took on responsibility for reconstructing the Castillo. Today, it houses the Canary Isles Museum of Emigrants. The Guanapay volcano offers a magnificent view of Teguise and surrounding countryside. A visit is well worth the effort. Open 10.00–17.00 hrs, Sat and Sun until 16.00 hrs.

★ Galería La Villa

An interesting arts and crafts centre in Teguise, on Plaza Clavijo y Fajardo, 4: the Heidi Bucher art gallery, a bookshop, Talia fashions, IslaViva (holiday houses in the country, 928 84 57 23). Tues–Fri 10.30-13.30, 17.00–19.30 hrs, Sun 10.00–14.00 hrs. Tel. 928 84 56 63.

⅋ Restaurante La Galería

La Galería is at Calle Nueva, no. 8, the street leading off the main square: tapas, vegetarian dishes, chili con carne, home-made cake. Live jazz on the last Friday of each month, from 20.30 hrs. Open from 10.00 hrs. Closed on Saturday.

⅋ Restaurante Ikarus

Excellent, top-quality restaurant. Open Tues-Sat from 19.00 hrs. Tel. 928 84 53 32.

⃗ Fiesta

Fiesta de Nuestra Señora del Carmen on 16th July, and the Fiesta de Rancho de Pascua on 24th December, a Christmas experience.

GALERÍA LA VILLA

The Galería La Villa, on the Plaza Clavijo y Fajardo, 4, in Teguise, is a storehouse of fine arts, an oasis of beautiful things, states, and dreams, unique on Lanzarote and a must for any interested visitor.

As you go in, you will find the exhibition rooms of the Heidi Bucher gallery. Heidi Bucher is an internationally renowned artist, who was born in 1926 in Winterthur and who died in Brunnen in 1993. She came to fame in Canada and California in the 1970s. In Switzerland Heidi Bucher became known for her skinning happenings and skin rooms.

Opposite the Heidi Bucher gallery is the exhibition and sales room of Talia-Moda Femenina. This offers designer fashions for women with a taste for the special, with the finest of materials: silks, linens, and cottons, made to measure. The shop is said to have the the most persuasive form of seduction since the fig-leaf (Tel./Fax 928 84 56 57).

At the centre of the building you will find Leo Libros y su Espacio, a bookshop with a book ordering department it would be hard to equal. You can browse and take your time choosing holiday reading. There is a wide selection, books on Lanzarote and the other Canary Isles, and also designer bookshelves that you can order here and have sent home, plus reading-lamps, bookmarks, accessories and anything and everything to do with books (Tel./Fax 928 84 56 63).

The Galería La Villa houses the office of Isla Viva – Casas en el campo. People looking for an idyll, for tranquillity, nature, tradition, relaxation and comfort have come to the right place here. The office is an agency for old restored country houses where you can spend a really individualistic holiday (Tel. 928 84 57 23. Fax 928 84 57 61).

Tiagua

The town is famous for its well-preserved windmills. Another sight worth seeing is the museum of local history and agriculture, the Villa Agrícola El Patio.

★ Museo Agrícola

The Museo Agrícola El Patio in Tiagua is a local museum well worth a visit, which shows how the Lanzaroteños live and work. On display are a variety of corn mills, traditional architecture, a completely furnished farmers' dwelling, an exhibition of photographs and much more. You can try the house's own wines in the wine room. When you get to the village of Tiagua, drive in the direction of the windmills. Mon–Fri 10.00–17.30 hrs, Sat 10.00–14.30 hrs. Closed on Sundays.

Tías

The little town divided by the motorway is the administrative seat of Puerto del Carmen.

⌗ Tienda Verde

Well-stocked whole food and organic produce shop, opposite the pharmacy. Open Mon–Fri 8.30–13.30 and 16.30–19.30, Sat 10.00–13.30 hrs.

🏃 Fiesta

Fiesta de Nuestra Señora del Carmen 16th July.

Museo Agrícola in Tiagua

MUSEO AGRÍCOLA EL PATIO

One trip you absolutely must make is to Tiagua, to the museum of local history and agriculture, the Museo Agrícola El Patio, at the geographical centre of Lanzarote. You will be surprised at the beautiful museum complex waiting for you here, a whole little village in itself where you can see fir yourself 150 years of farming tradition, and imagine how people lived. This is an authentic and original piece of Lanzarote where you can stroll, relax, and enjoy.

In 1845, impoverished farmers began cultivating new fertile land here, that belonged to the count de la Quinta, Don Francisco Ponta y Llorena. A hundred years later, this was the largest and best-kept estate on Lanzarote, with 25 farmers and 20 camels working it. In 1994, the estate was opened to the public as a museum, and only two years later it was awarded the top official tourism prize.

There is really plenty to see here: two ethnographical museum rooms with a completely furnished farmers' dwelling dating back to the early 20th century; several mills that you can go into; antique tilling implements; a collection of pottery reconstructed on the basis of finds from excavations on the estate itself; a comprehensive exhibition of photographs; and last but not least, the magnificent traditional architecture, which is a sight in itself.

You will also find the domestic animals that are typical of the island, plus a grape-press, a bodega and the wine room, where you can taste and buy the excellent and exclusive El Patio wine. Muscatel, malvasia and a good tinto (red wine) are all on offer. To help it down, you can eat the goats' cheese of the house.

Open Monday to Friday, 10.00–17.30 hrs, and Saturday, 10.00–14.30 hrs. Closed on Sundays. Tel./Fax 928 52 91 34.

Tinajo

Capital of the region of the same name, which includes a part of the Timanfaya National Park. Has about 3,000 inhabitants and is situated between Mancha Blanca and La Santa. The church bears a sun dial from the year 1881.

★ Centro de Visitantes

Half-way between the Ruta de los Volcanes and Tinajo you will find the Mancha Blanca Visitors and Information Centre, which is of interest to anyone wanting to know about volcanism in general, or about the origins of the Canary Islands, the eruptions on Lanzarote and Timanfaya National Park in particular. Open daily 19.00–17.00, admission free. There is a video show about 30 minutes long and well worth seeing, every hour on the hour. The Centro also houses a volcanology museum, a library and very special shop, the only place where you can find exclusive souvenirs of the National Park, along with gifts and books. Tel. 928 84 02 38.

⚡ Fiesta

Fiesta de Nuestra Señora de los Volcanes 15th September.

CENTRO DE VISITANTES E INTERPRETACIÓN
DE MANCHA BLANCA

Lanzarote's great sensation is without doubt the Timanfaya National Park, with its Ruta de los Volcanes. But before driving into the National Park, we suggest you visit the Centro de Visitantes, situated half-way between the Ruta de los Volcanes and Tinajo.

This is a visitors' centre where you can get all the information you need on volcanism in general and on the origins of the Lanzarotean volcanos in particular. Other topics are geodynamics, ecosystems, the coastal region of the park, La Geria, the flora and fauna, and an interpretation of the immediate vicinity of the Centro de Visitantes, which was built in a sea of lava.

After a visit to the Centre, even "volcanology beginners" can spot the special features of the National Park more easily, and understand and enjoy it better.

The Centre has been awarded a number of architecture prizes, and has a half-hour audiovision show, a library and a grotto where the acoustic effect of an eruption is simulated. It is easy to imagine how the people of Lanzarote must have felt when the real eruptions occurred.

A shop of a very special kind is integrated into the museum. This offers you not only exclusive mementoes of the National Park, but also very tastefully selected souvenirs and interesting books.

Open daily 9.00–17.00 hrs, audiovision 9.00–16.00 hrs. Admission free. Tel. 928 84 02 38.

Uga

This sleepy, African looking spot is situated on the edge of the volcanic landscape between Mácher and Yaiza. The dromedaries that carry tourists to Timanfaya are bred here. Uga has an exotic air, especially in the early afternoon when the dromedaries return from work and are herded along the streets. Uga is the home of the most famous school (along with Telde on Gran Canaria) of *Lucha canaria*, Canary wrestling.

⑪ Ahumadería Uga

On a level with Uga, right next to the main road between Mácher and Yaiza, you will find the excellent Uga salmon-smoking plant, which is highly recommended (house number 4). The quality of the salmon is second to none. The fish are imported from Norway or Scotland and finely smoked, and then sold for 4,600 Ptas. per kilogram. A minimum of half a kilogram must be purchased. Special travel packaging. The Ahumadería is open Tues–Fri from 10.00–13.00 hrs. Sat from 10.00–14.00 hrs. Tel. 928 83 01 32.

⑪ Restaurante Gregorio

Gregorio restaurant is a typical Canarian inn. We especially recommend the kid's meat (carbito frito), the tapas and the Canarian stew (puchero, but only on Sundays). Closed on Tuesdays.

🐎 Lanzarote a Caballo

Between Uga and Mácher, at about kilometre 17, is the stud farm Lanzarote a Caballo. This provides introductory and jumping courses and rides, for beginners too. Tel. 928 83 03 14.

🎆 Fiesta

Fiesta de San Isidro 15th May.

Yaiza

The village is situated to the west of Arrecife between Uga and the Salinas de Janubio and is home to about 2,000 inhabitants. With its white houses punctuated solitary palms, Yaiza is the most impressive village in Lanzarote (along with Haría). It has already been considered twice in the annual election of Spain's most beautiful village. Yaiza has an African feeling about it. The facades of some of the houses show that the more affluent islanders live here. Looking to the north, one's glance falls on the Timanfaya national park and the Fire Mountains. The parish church Nuestra Señora de los Remedios dates from the 18th century. The bar on the road leading through is authentic.

★ Montañas del Fuego o de Timanfaya

If you start from Yaiza and drive five kilometres into the National Park, you will come to Timanfaya, at the foot of which caravans of dromedaries await tour-

ists. From here, you can ride up the Fire Mountains and survey the unique "moonscape"

★ Ruta de Los Volcanes
The Ruta de Los Volcanes starts just a few kilometres after the dromedary caravans at Timanfaya. From here, you have to pay admission, which includes a round bus trip through the volcanic landscape, with a commentary on the various volcanic phenomena. Open from 9.00–18.00 hrs.

★ Galería Yaiza
The Yaiza gallery is worth a visit. One can buy pictures and pottery there; various exhibitions are held. Open from 17.00–19.00 hrs. Sunday closed.

⊮ Restaurante La Era
La Era is a farmhouse more than 300 years old. César Manrique and Luis Ibáñez restored it and converted it into the most original Canarian restaurant, where some typical Canarian dishes are served. The garden is also worth seeing. Open from 13.00–23.00 hrs.

⊮ Restaurante El Campo
Excellent restaurant with Canary Isles and international cuisine. The fish and meat are fresh daily. Beautiful sun terrace. The restaurant is just before the football pitch. Open daily 9.00–23.00 hrs. Tel. 928 83 03 44.

🏛 Hotel Finca de las Salinas
The Finca de las Salinas is a country hotel, providing some of the best accommodation on Lanzarote. Calle La Cuesta, 17. Tel. 928 83 03 25. Fax 928 83 03 29.

⫷ Fiesta
Fiesta de Nuestra Señora de los Remedios 8th September.

PARQUE NACIONAL DE TIMANFAYA

If one travels 5 km on from Yaiza in the National park, one comes to the Timanfaya, where caravans of dromedaries wait at the foot of the mountains for tourists. From here you can ride into the Fire Mountains and experience the unique "moon landscape". Here you will find all kinds of volcanic manifestations, which were created in the period of eruptions 1730–1736. It is well worth visiting the Fire mountains just to see the volcanoes' many nuances of colour, their shades changing as the trade wind clouds drift by. A few kilometres from the caravans of dromedaries the *Ruta de los Volcanes* begins. From this point on it is necessary to pay an entry fee. It is open daily from 9.00–18.00 hrs. A round trip by bus through the volcanic landscape is included in the entry fee. The individual volcanic manifestations are explained during this tour.

It is two kilometres from the pay booth to the Islote de Hilario. This is the centre of the active volcanic landscape. The earth is hot. By way of demonstration a piece of gorse is put into a natural opening in the earth to a depth of about half a metre – it soon starts to burn. Water that is shaken into metal pipes (which are left in the earth) vaporizes in seconds and shoots out of the earth in fountains of steam. These natural spectacles are performed continously by one of the park employees. The earth's temperature is already 400 °C six metres down.

The hermit Hilario is said to have lived at the Islote de Hilario for 50 years. His only companion was a dromedary. Hilario is said to have planted a fig tree which never bore fruit, because, according to legend, the blossom could not feed on the flames.

Manrique built the *El Diablo* restaurant at the Islote de Hilario; its simple lines mean it is well integrated into the landscape. Only materials such as stone, metal and glass were used due to the high temperature of the earth. From the generously proportioned dining room, one has a wonderful panoramic view right across the volcanoes to the sea. It is a thorough pleasure to while away a little time here.

The kitchen is something of a surprise – it is powered, at least in part, by the volcano. A large grill above an opening of about 6 m depth, is powered by the earth's warmth. The reading on the grill is 300 °C. The ideal grilling temperature.

Yé

The little town is in the north, between Máguez and Mirador del Río, at the foot of Monte Corona.

★ Mirador del Río

Mirador del Río is a look-out point on the island's north cape. 479 metres up, it towers over the islands like an eyrie. Looking northwards through a panorama window, you can see La Graciosa. Montaña Clara and Alegranza. Manrique was responsible for the conversion of the former artillery store Baterías del Río. Daily 10.00–18.00 hrs.

MIRADOR DEL RÍO

Mirador means vantage point, look-out, oriel. Mirador del Río is an oriel on the north cap of the island, 479 m high, it stands like an eyrie in solitary splendour above Graciosa. The view across to the islands Graciosa, Montaña Clara and Alegranza is fantastic.

It was none other than Manrique who was responsible for the conversion of the former artillery store *Baterías del Río*. However, the idea came from an utopian project by the Madrid architect Fernando Higueras, who wanted to build a village into the mountains above the beach of Famara. It was to be a village with lifts to the beach, small groups of bungalows in the mountain wall and tunnel streets. Manrique felt uneasy about the frequent power cuts in Lanzarote which could be a result and so the project was never carried out. But it did give Manrique the idea for Mirador del Río.

He had the mountain dug up, built a restaurant in the valley, had two rounded hill tops created above the great space; they were covered in earth, the grass grew on them. Looking towards the north, one can see the off shore islands through a large panoramic window.

If one approaches from the south, either via Haría and Yé, or Arrieta and Yé, the street ends by a wrought-iron emblem, before a wall of hills disguised in natural stone. It is open daily from 10.00–18.00 hrs. By going through a short corridor one can get into the great hall, which is made less severe by two of Manrique's sculptures hanging from the twin domes.

2. BEACHES

The coast of Lanzarote measures 194.6 km. There are 87 beaches on this stretch of coastline. 28 of them are white or golden sand, 33 are black sand, the rest are mixed or stoney. Only 36 of the beaches are used for touristic purposes. Six of the beaches are mediumly well frequented, only two are crowded. It is still possible to find a quiet spot. Nude sun bathing is tolerated, but only done on the quieter beaches.

Sun loungers, sun shades, surf boards and peddle boats can be hired at the Playa Blanca near Puerto del Carmen (not to be confused with the village Playa Blanca in the south), the island's most crowded beach. Traders sometimes come by with drinks and other things. Bars and restaurants are nearby.

You can only reach the quieter beaches by car. There are no traders there and you have to take your own food.

Just one warning – Don't swim out too far, the current are unpredictable and can be dangerous. If you want to swim long distances, swim parallel to the coast.

Playa Bastian

This large sandy beach is in the south of Costa Teguise. Shade is provided by palm-trees.

Playa Blanca by Puerto del Carmen

Is situated in front of the tourist centre of Puerto del Carmen and is a light, wide sand beach about 2,500 m in length. It is the most popular beach. Bars, restaurants and apartments are not much further than 100 m away. The beach and the water are clean. The beach is particularly suitable for children.

Towards Playa Quemada, in the south west of Puerto del Carmen, there are small, undisturbed beaches and bays.

Playa Blanca in the south

This is also the name of the late fishing village which is becoming a tourist settlement. The beach is actually very small, always quite full, with a nice view across to Fuerteventura. The beach is next to Playa Blanca's bank promenade, where there are many bars and restaurants.

Playa de la Arena

Black sand beach in the south of Playa Quemadas. At low tide it is easy to reach along the shoreline, but at high tide you will have to take the footpath over the rocks.

Playa de la Cantería

It is the most north easterly beach, situated to the west of Orzola. It is mostly windy and cool. Dangerous current, one should not swim outside the bay.

Playa de las Cucharas

The beach is at the centre of Costa Teguise, between the Hotel Las Salinas and the Hotel Teguise Playa. There is mostly a strong offshore wind, which has

made the beach a centre for windsurfers. Plenty of places to eat and drink.

Playa Dorada

Artificial sand beach in the east of Playa Blanca, between the Hotel Playa Dorada and the Centro Comercial Papagayo. The Playa Dorada is very suitable for families with children. Sunloungers and sunshades can be hired. There is a restaurant and sanitary facilities.

Playa de Famara

Playa de Famara is amongst the most beautiful beaches on Lanzarote. However, there is a continuous strong on-shore wind. Caution is advised when bathing, the current is strong. Don't swim out too far, you could be swept out to the open sea! The coast of Playa de Famara is suitable for surfing and wave riding. The beach stretches more than one kilometre before the Risco de Famara, a steep cliff wall. The holiday town Famara can be found behind the beach, the village of La Caleta is situated to the west.

Playa Flamingo

The Playa Flamingo is an artificial beach in the west of Playa Blanca, protected from the open sea by two breakwaters. Particularly suitable for children. Sunloungers and sunshades can be hired. Plenty of restaurants to choose from.

Playa de la Garita

Here on the east coast, to the south and north of Arrieta, there is a series of small beaches, some of which are hard to get to. Here you can be undisturbed. The largest is the Playa de la Garita which is right by Arrieta.

Playa de Janubio

Situated in the south west of the island, near the Salinas of Janubio. This black sand beach is not used much. Be careful of the current. Swimming here can be highly dangerous!

Playa de Matagorda

Is the continuation of the Playa de los Pocillos. The beach alternates between sand and reefs.

Playa Mojón Blanco & Caleta del Mero

Driving towards Orzola from Los Jameos del Agua, just before Orzola you will come across two white dune areas, spreading inland from the sea. There is no shade on the beaches.

Playas de Papagayo

About 4 km from the village of Playa Blanca there is a series of sand bays around the Punta de Papagayo, the most southernly point of Lanzarote. The beaches begin at the Punta del Águila, where the Castillo de las Coloradas stands. The beach here is a little stoney with black sand. The light sand beaches, the most beautiful in Lanzarote begin a little further on after some hills and cliffs. They are flat and the water is as clear as glass. These beaches are:

At 400 metres, the Playa Mujeres is the longest beach. It can be reached directly by car, though parking is only allowed on the designated, guarded carpark.

Playa del Caletón and Playa de las Ahogaderas can both be reached on foot from Playa Mujeres.

Playa del Pozo is about 300 metres long, with archeological excavations, where San Marcial del Rubicón, the remains of a Norman township from 1402, can be found.

Playa de la Cera follows Playa del Pozo.

Playa de Papagayo is a semicircular bay where fragments of the former village of El Papagayo still stand. There is a small restaurant. The beach can be used for nude bathing. A carpark has been built above it, by the houses.

Caleta del Congrio lies just around the Punta de Papagayo,

and can be reached on foot from the Playa Puerto Muelas.

Playa de Puerto Muelas also has a car-park, and a camp-site.

This region was declared a natural monument and bird protection zone in 1994. There is a road leading into this protected region, closed by a barrier at the old lime-kiln. A charge is made for driving in by car.

Playa de los Pocillos

Playa de los Pocillos is situated in front of the urbanisation of Los Pocillos, this beach is the north easterly extension of the Playa Blanca near Puerto del Carmen and stretches about 2 km. Good for surfing, running and bathing. Less crowded than the Playa Blanca beach.

Playa del Reducto

Arrecifas municipal beach south of the Avenida Fred Olsen, located in a broad, wind-sheltered bay.

Playa del Risco

This is a large, secluded sandy beach in the exteme north of Lanzarote, below the Mirador del Río. It can only be reached on foot, along a strenuous mountain path. There is a difference in altitude of around 400 metres to tackle. The path begins to the south of the Mirador del Río, on the road towards Guinate.

■

Playa Mojón Blanco & Caleta del Mero

3. THE BEST TRIPS ROUND THE ISLAND

Here are some brief notes as suggestions for six routes. If you hire a car, you can manage each of the suggested trips in a day. If you try to see the whole island in one day, you will have to drive more than 300 kilometres. To explore Lanzarote thoroughly, you should leave yourself at least two days, if not more. Our suggested routes start at Playa Blanca, Puerto del Carmen and Costa Teguise, where most holiday-makers have their accomodation. For descriptions of the individual towns and villages, please refer to the chapter on Towns and Sights.

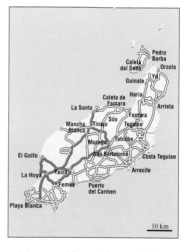

Starting at Playa Blanca

South route: Playa Blanca – Salinas de Janubio – Los Hervideros – El Golfo (to the green lagoon and the fishing-village) – Yaiza – Timanfaya (dromedary ride) – (first to the Centro de Visitantes) Mancha Blanca – (back to the Ruta de Los Volcanes) Montañas del Fuego – Tinajo (you could also make a detour to La Santa) – Tiagua (Museo Agrícola El Patio) – Tao

– Mozaga (Casa Museo y Monumento al Campesino) – El Grifo (Museo del Vino) – Masdache – La Geria – Uga – Femés – Las Breñas – Playa Blanca (approx. 160 km incl. detours) – Our advice: Take an extra day for the Papagayo beaches, and half a day each for the Montañas del Fuego and the Museo Agrícola El Patio in Tiagua.

North route: Playa Blanca – Yaiza – Tías – San Bartolomé – Mozaga (Casa Museo y Monumento al Campesino) – La Caleta – Teguise (possible detour to the Castillo de Santa Bár-

10 km

Starting at Puerto del Carmen

South route: Puerto del Carmen – Mácher – (possible detour to Playa Quemada) – Femés – Las Breñas – Playa Blanca – Salinas de Janubio – Los Hervideros – El Golfo (to the green lagoon and the fishing village) – Yaiza – Timanfaya (dromedary ride) – (first the Centro de Visitantes) Mancha Blanca – (back to the Ruta de los

10 km

bara, Museo del Emigrante Canario) – Los Valles – Haría (Museo de Miniaturas) – Máguez – Guinate (Parque Tropical) – Yé – Mirador del Río – Cueva del los Verdes – Los Jameos del Agua (with a possible detour to Orzola) – Punta de Mujeres – Arrieta – Mala – Guatiza (Jardín de Cactus) – (possible detour to the Costa Teguise) – Tahiche (Fundación César Manrique) – Arrecife – then straight back to Playa Blanca via Mácher and Yaiza (approx. 180 km including detours) – Our advice: Spread this route across two days. Cueva de los Verdes, Los Jameos del Agua and Jardín de Cactus can easily take a day.

■

Volcanes) Montañas del Fuego – Tinajo (possible detour to La Santa) – Tiagua (Museo Agrícola El Patio) – Tao – Mozaga (Casa Museo y Monumento al Campesino) – El Grifo (Museo del Vino) – Masdache – La Geria – Uga – Mácher – Puerto del Carmen (approx. 160 km including detours) – Our advice: Take an extra day for the Papagayo

166

beaches, and half a day each for the Montañas del Fuego and the Museo Agrícola El Patio in Tiagua.

North route: Puerto del Carmen – Tías – San Bartolomé – Mozaga (Casa Museo y Monumento al Campesino) – La Caleta – Teguise (with a possible detour to the Castillo de Santa Bárbara, Museo del Emigrante Canario) – Los Valles – Haría (Museo de Miniaturas) – Máguez – Guinate (Parque Tropical) – Yé – Mirador del Río – Cueva del los Verdes – Los Jameos del Agua (possible detour to Orzola) – Punta de Mujeres – Arrieta – Mala – Guatiza (Jardín de Cactus) – (possible detour to the Costa Teguise) – Tahiche (Fundación César Manrique) – Arrecife – Puerto del Carmen (approx. 160 km including detours) – Our advice: Spread this route across two

days. Cueva de los Verdes, Los Jameos del Agua and Jardín de Cactus can easily take a day.

Starting at Costa Teguise

South route: Costa Teguise – Tahiche (Fundación César Manrique) – San Bartolomé – Mozaga (Casa Museo y Monumento al Campesino) – El Grifo (Museo del Vino) – Masdache – La Geria – Uga – Femés – Las Breñas – Playa Blanca – Salinas de Janubio – Los Hervideros – El Golfo (to the green lagoon and the fishing village) – Yaiza – Timanfaya (dromedary ride) – (first the Centro de Visitantes) Mancha Blanca – (back to the Ruta de los Volcanes) Montañas del Fuego – Tinajo (possible detour to La Santa) – Tiagua (Museo Agrícola El Patio) – Tao – Mozaga – San Bartolomé –

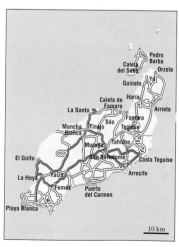

Arrecife – Costa Teguise (approx. 180 km including detours) – Our advice: Take an extra day for the Papagayo beaches, and half a day each for the Montañas del Fuego and the Museo Agrícola El Patio in Tiagua.

North route: Costa Teguise – Tahiche (Fundación César Manrique) – Teguise (with a possible detour to the Castillo de Santa Bárbara, Museo del Emigrante Canario) – Los Valles – Haría (Museo de Miniaturas) – Máguez – Guianate (Parque Tropical) – Yé – Mirador del Río – Cueva del los Verdes – Los Jameos del Agua (with a possible detour to Orzola) – Punta de Mujeres – Arrieta – Mala – Guatiza (Jardín de Cactus) – Costa Teguise (approx. 120 km including detours) – Our advice: Cueva de los Verdes, Los

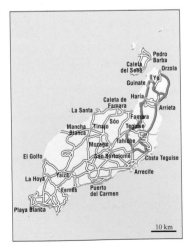

Jameos del Agua and Jardín de Cactus can easily fill a whole day.

Tour operators also offer excursions. You can go on coach tours in the south and north, or an excursion to Fuerteventura. You can fly to Morocco or explore the country side away from the roads on jeep safaris. You can go out to sea for deep-sea fishing or sailing, and you can ride in a submarine. Ask

your tour operator or a travel agent.

May we recommend our road-map for your excursions: **The Map of Lanzarote**, with brief descriptions of the most important places & sights, and all the information you need.

■

4. TRAVELLING WITH CHILDREN

Children who love sun, sand, and sea will love Lanzarote. The Papagayo beaches, the beaches by Puerto del Carmen, Los Pocillos and Matagorda, the Playa Flamingo, the Playa Dorada and the Playa Blanca in Playa Blanca, are all particularly suitable for children and infants. They have broad, light-coloured sandy beaches, and the water is relatively shallow along the edge. Apart from the Papagayo beaches, they all offer you plenty of places to sit and eat or drink, and plenty of shade. Doctors advise against letting children play out in the sun too long, and they should never be naked, and always have their heads covered. With the refreshing trade wind, it is easy to underestimate the intensity of the sun's rays.

Children are welcomed warmly in almost all the hotels, there are games and playgrounds available, and children's activities are provided to keep the little ones busy.

Attractions your children will love:

Agua Lanza is a swimmers' paradise, with a lot of different water slides. You will find it below the golf course on the Costa Teguise. Open daily 10.00–17.00 hrs.

You can ride out to sea in the aquascope and watch the underwater world. The boats are safe and air-conditioned. One aquascope leaves from the harbour at Puerto del Carmen, and one from Playa Blanca. There is a round trip every half hour from 10.00 hrs onwards.

The Castillo de Santa Bárbara above Teguise is a real castle with a drawbridge. It houses the museum of Emigrants. Open 10.00–17.00 hrs, or until 16.00 hrs Sat and Sun.

A walk round a cave will thrill your children. The Cueva de los Verdes to the north of Punta de Mujeres is open 10.00–18.00 hrs.

On your way from Yaiza to the Fire Mountains, you will first come to Timanfaya, where the whole family can ride up the mountain on dromedaries.

Spend a day on the "pirate ship" Marea Errota, a two-masted wooden schooner 24 metres in length. The pirate games will give you and your children hours

of fun. You will also be given food and drink on board. A free service will pick you up from your hotel to take you to the Marea Errota in Playa Blanca. For further information, ask your hotel or apartment reception.

The Museo Agrícola El Patio in Tiagua is also an ideal place for families with children. This is a large area with the animals typical of a Lanzerotean farm, where you can let your children play in peace while you relax with excellent wine and goat's cheese. This is also a local history museum, where there is a lot to look at showing you how the Lanzaroteños live and work. Open Mon–Fri 10.00–17.30 hrs. Sat 10.00–14.30 hrs. Closed on Sundays.

There is pony-riding for children at Rancho Texas in Puerto del Carmen, and at Lanzarote a Caballo between Uga and Mácher. Both riding stables have the same opening hours: 10.00–14.00 and 16.00–19.00 hrs daily in winter, and 10.00–14.00 and 17.00–20.00 hrs in summer. For further information, ask the reception where you are staying.

How about showing your children cycling parrots? Visit the Parque Tropical in Guinate. This is an exotic bird park with over 300 different species of bird. Open daily 10.00–17.00 hrs.

In Puerto Calero, one of the finest yachting marinas in the Canary Isles, there are large yachts to look at, and you can go for a ride in a submarine. Submarine Safaris offer an underwater trip that goes down 25–30 metres, daily 9.00–19.00 hrs. Inquiry directly at the Submarine Safaris office at the harbour.

Wolfgang Borsich / Jan Černý

Mrs Lisa

Children's holiday reading:
MS LISA. A picture book for children from 3 to 99 years. The book tells the story of a dog that lives by the sea.

5. GENERAL TRAVEL INFORMATION

This chapter provides information especially relating to Lanzarote, and sometimes to all the Canary Isles, in alphabetical order. Addresses, timetables etc. may change after going to press, so although we have taken great care to ensure the information is correct, we cannot guarantee it. The information is up-to-date at the time of printing, and is updated in each new edition.

Airline

IBERIA: Arrecife, Avda. Rafael Gonzáles Negrin, 2, Tel. 928 81 53 75.

Airport: Tel. 928 81 14 50.

Bathing

The temperature of the water varies over the year between 18 and 24 °C. The currents are sometimes dangerous and you are advised to swim along the coastline, never far out. Nudist bathing is tolerated on some beaches, it is not actually allowed by Spanish law. Do not underestimate the sun's power, especially on the first few days. The refreshing trade winds mean that its effects are not always obvious.

Canarias Spezial

If you want to keep away from the large tourist centres, and prefer to spend your holiday in a rustic finca in the country, or a cottage by the sea or a specially selected romantic hotel, we recommend the German agency CANARIAS SPEZIAL REISEN, which offers more than 400 houses and other accommodation on all seven of the Canary Isles, of every type and size, in any style, from simple to luxurious. Houses and other accommodation for up to twelve persons, flights and hire cars can be booked, if you want a hotel service (cook, baby-sitter etc.), this can be arranged. The agency has a separate catalogue for each of the seven Canary Isles. For further information, inquire at: CANARIAS SPEZIAL REISEN GmbH & Co. KG, Konrad-Adenauer-Str. 44, D-69221 Dossenheim. Tel. 049 / 062 21 / 86 32 53, 049 / 0 62 21 / 86 98 65. Fax 049 / 062 21 / 86 32 18.

Carnival

On Lanzarote, they celebrate carnival for weeks and

weeks. Shrove Monday sees the first great procession in Arrecife. On Ash Wednesday, they bury the "sardine" according to an old heathen custom, with weeping and moaning from a black-clad people. After the procession, the sardine is burnt and its ashes scattered in the sea. The following weekend, there is a procession in Puerto del Carmen, along the coast road, between the Hotel San Antonio and the Hotel Fariones. In the villages, carnival is not celebrated until after this. The last carnival procession goes through Playa Blanca.

Chemists

Chemist is *farmacia* in Spanish and is signposted by a red or green cross. The emergency services alternate. Details of services on Sunday and during the night are listed on every chemist's window *(Farmacia de Guardia)*. They are open the usual business hours: Mon–Fri 9.00–13.00 hrs and 16.00–20.00 hrs, on Sat 9.00–13.00 hrs. Those insured under the NHS (or state medicine scheme) only have to pay a contribution towards costs if they can show a medical insurance record card *(talonario)*. A medication for something is called *un medicamento contra*.

Some common ailments in Spanish:

cold: *resfriado*
constipation: *estreñimiento*
diabetes: *diabetes*
diarrhoea: *diarrea*
headache: *dolores de cabeza*
heartburn: *ardor del estómago*
indigestion: *trastornos*
influenza: *gripe*
insect bites: *picados de insectos*
insomnia: *insomnio*
nasal catarrh: *catarro nasal*
nausea: *náuseas*
rheumatism: *reumatismo*
sea sickness: *mareo*
sore throat: *dolores de garganta*
stomachache: *dolores de estómago*
sunburn: *quemadura solar*
sunstroke: *insolación*
tonsillitis: *amigdalitis, anginas*

Some medicines and medical supplies

aspirin: *aspirina*
bandage: *venda*
bicarbonate of soda: *bicarbonato sódico*
blood-staunching (styptic) preparation: *cortasangre*
burns ointment: *pomada para quemaduras*
charcoal tablets: *pastillas de carbón*
circulatory preparation (vasopressor): *remedio circulatorio*
condoms: *preservativos*
cough medicine: *jarabe pectoral*
disinfectant: *desinfectante*
dressing: *vendajes*
eyedrops: *gotas para los ojos*
gauze bandage: *venda de gasa*
healing ointment: *ungüento*
laxative: *laxante*
pain-killers: *analgésico*
sedatives: *calmante*
sleeping drug: *somnifero*
sticking plaster: *esparadrapo*

temperature-lowering (antipyretic) preparation: *antipirético*

Consulate

Luis Morote 6–3 (apartado 2020)
Puerto de la Luz
La Palmas
35007 Gran Canaria
Tel. 928 26 25 08/12/16
There is no Irish Consulate on the Canaries.

Credit cards

Hotels, some restaurants, shops an car rental firms usually accept credit cards, though this still cannot be relied on completely. It is not customary to accept Eurocheques in restaurants and shops.

Customs duty

The Canary Isles have special status, so they were not integrated into the European Customs Union.

When returning home, note the following regulations:

Importing the furs of many animal species, crocodile leather and ivory is completely banned.

The following limits apply to persons over 15 years of age: 250 g coffee or 100 g instant coffee, 100 g tea or 40 g tea extract, 0.25 l eau de toilette or 50 g perfume. For persons over 17 years: 2 l spirits under 22%, 1 l spirits over 22% or 2 l wine, 200 cigarettes or 50 cigars or 250 g tobacco.

Doctors

There are good doctors for you to consult, though you may have a long way to go. In emergencies, your tour guide or hotel receptionist will help you find a doctor. In large hotels and apartment complexes there are contract doctors who hold regular clinics, which can also be attended by tourists who are not residents.

If you are dependent on particular medicines, you are advised to keep a supply. It is also a good idea to have a travel kit containing medicines for travel sickness, sunburn, headaches, diarrhoea and so on. No inoculations are required before entering the Canary Islands. Injections are not given by doctors, but by their assistants or *practicantes*.

When a patient needs to be hospitalized, it is usual for a member of the family to give extra assistance. Doctors' bills generally have to be paid immediately.

Drinking water

Tap and well water is not suitable for drinking without boiling it beforehand. You can buy mineral water in most supermarkets. You should try to drink a lot of it to compensate for the loss of fluid (through sweating). Water is in short supply on all the islands, especially Lanzarote, Fuerteventura and El Hierro. You are asked to use it sparingly.

Driving

The main roads are good on all the islands, though in some places they are overloaded. Off the main routes you will come across shingle roads and unmake tracks, some of which can only be negotiated by jeep. If you have a breakdown or an accident, you can obtain assistance from the *Policía Municipal* within towns and villages or the *Guardia Civil* in the countryside. It is illegal for a private vehicle to tow another vehicle. There are heavy fines for overtaking where overtaking is prohibited and for exceeding the speed limit. This is 90 km/h on country roads and usually 40 km/h within town limits. Seatbelts are mandatory outside town limits. Fines generally have to be paid on the spot. Traffic regulations are similar to those at home. In Spain, the "weaker" road user is always in the right. Remember to drive on the right. Vehicles coming from the right have right of way over vehicles coming from the left, even at roundabouts. Use your horn before blind bends and before overtaking. Drivers often use hand signals to indicate turning: horizontal arm to turn left, vertical arm to turn right.

Emergency calls

If you do not know the language, ask for help from the nearest hotel or apartment reception. They will be glad to help.

Ambulances: Tel. 928 81 22 22
Guardia Civil: Tel. 062

Excursions

Whatever island you are on, there is a wide range of excursions for you to choose from: island tours, photographic and jeep safaris, one-day voyages, deep-sea angling, folklore evenings, one-day and serveral-day trips to neighbouring islands, even a day excursion to Morocco. Excursions are organized by both local travel agents and by tour operators. Package tourists are usually given information on excursions while they are enjoying their "welcoming cocktail".

Ferry connections

We recommend the Fred Olsen line.

Fuerteventura – Lanzarote
With the *Buganvilla Ferry*
Playa Blanca – Corralejo
8.00, 10.00, 14.00, 18.00 hrs.
Corralejo – Playa Blanca
9.00. 11.00, 17.00, 19.00 hrs.

With the *Volcán de Tindaya*
Playa Blanca – Corralejo
9.00, 11.00, 17.00, 19.00 hrs.
Corralejo – Playa Blanca
8.00, 10.00, 14.00, 18.00 hrs.

A ferry goes to **Lobos** from Corralejo at 10.00 hrs. The return trip is at 17.00 hrs in winter, and 18.00 hrs in summer, or as agreed.

Garbage

Please take your rubbish with you, so the beaches will stay clean in the coming years.

Going home

The times of charter flights back can change at short notice, so you should check with your tour operator three days before your departure. You will only have a claim to the flight you have booked if it is confirmed.

Hire cars

You will find car hire firms in all towns and holiday resorts. Small and medium-sized cars and of-road vehicles are available. Full comprehensive insurance is compulsory with most firms, and if you cause an accident, you may have to cover some of the cost yourself. Towing costs are always charged to the hirer. Cars that are not off-road vehicles may only be driven on asphalt roads. If you ignore this regulation and drive across country, you will be liable for any damage caused.

Watch out for the small print in contracts – there should be a translation available. This may include a clause that the vehicle must not be used in tidal zones. Even jeeps are not built to withstand salt water. If you drive through sea water, the hire firm may claim compensation.

Before you sign the contract check that the car is roadworthy and inspect it for sign of any accident damage. Check that there is a spare wheel and a car-jack.

Not very many motorbikes and mopeds are available for hiring (a helmet is compulsory if you do hire one).

There are bicycle hire firms, but the heat and strong winds can make cycling rather unpleasant.

Holiday season

Because of its mild climate, Fuerteventura is suitable for holidays all year round. The temperature of the water ranges from 18 °C in winter to 24 °C in summer. However, there may be cold and occasionally even rainy days in winter, whilst the summer can become unbearably hot, when the sirocco heats the air to a maximum of 50 °C and fills it with sand.

The most pleasant time of year is between May and July. The main holiday seasons are: the Christmas, Easter and summer holidays; October, November and February.

Hospital

The Hospital General de Lanzarote is in Arrecife, on the exit road to Arrecife–San Barto-lomé–Tinajo, at km 1.3. Tel. 928 80 17 52 and 928 80 16 36.

If you need medical attention, please also refer to the chapter on Towns and Sights.

Triste y sola está la novia. En
el Ayuntamiento de San Bartolome.

muchos novios la pretenden
y ninguno feliz la sabe hacer.

Language

In most cases Spanish is pronounced just as it is spelt. Here are the exceptions:

b is pronounced softly

c in front of i and e is pronounced th (cena – dinner)

ch is pronounced like ch in chair (coche – car)

d on the end of a word is pronounced only slightly or not at all (Madrid)

g in front of a, o, u is hard (like in good)

g in front of e, i is pronounced like a hard ck (Argentina)

gue, gui is pronounced ge, gi (as in Teguise)

güi is pronounced like gui (Güime)

h is not pronounced

j is pronounced like a hard ch (ajo – garlic)

ll is pronounced like ly (paella)

ñ is pronounced like ny (mañana – tomorrow)

qu is pronounced like a hard c (queso – cheese)

r are rolled (pero – but)

rr is stronger (perro – dog)

s is pronounced like a double ss

z is pronounced like a strong th

The vowels are always short. If words have an accent (último), it is always the letter with the accent which is stressed. The stress for words without accents which end in a vowel or n or s (febrero) is on the last but one syllable. If words end in other consonants (metal) the last syllable is given the emphasis.

Numbers

0	cero
1	uno (un) (una)
2	dos
3	tres
4	cuatro
5	cinco
6	seis
7	siete
8	ocho
9	nueve
10	diez
11	once
12	doce
13	trece
14	catorce
15	quince
16	dieciseis
17	diecisiete
18	dieciocho
19	diecinueve
20	veinte
21	veintiuno
30	treinta
31	treinta y uno
40	cuarenta
41	cuarenta y uno
50	cincuenta
51	cincuenta y uno
60	sesenta
61	sesenta y uno
70	setenta
71	setenta y uno
80	ochenta
81	ochenta y uno
90	noventa
91	noventa y uno
100	ciento (cien)
200	doscientos/as
300	trescientos/as
500	quinientos/as
1000	mil
2000	dos mil

Days

Monday: *lunes*
Tuesday: *martes*
Wednesday: *miércoles*
Thursday: *jueves*
Friday: *viernes*
Saturday: *sábado*
Sunday: *domingo*

Months

January: *enero*
February: *febrero*
March: *marzo*
April: *abril*
May: *mayo*
June: *junio*
July: *julio*
August: *agosto*
September: *septiembre*
October: *octubre*
November: *noviembre*
December: *diciembre*

Words and Phrases

Good morning/Good day
  Buenos días
Good afternoon
  Buenas tardes
Good evening/Good night
  Buenas noches
Goodbye – *Hasta la vista/*
  Adios
See you later – *Hasta luego*
Please – *por favor*
Thank you – *(muchas)*
  gracias
yes/no – *si/no*
Mr/Mrs/Miss
  señor/señora/señorita
Excuse me – *Perdone*
Do you speak English?
  ¿Habla Usted ingles?

Where is …?
  ¿Donde está …?
the street/the hotel
  la calle/el hotel
right – *derecha*
left – *isquierda*
above – *arriba*
below – *abajo*
Is there a … here?
  ¿Hay por aqui …?
toilet – *lavabó*
room – *habitación*
room with a bathroom
  habitación con baño
full board
  con pension completa
everything included
  todo incluido
How much is …?
  ¿Cuánto cuesta …?
bill – *la cuenta*
help – *socorro*
Where is a doctor/chemist?
  ¿Dónde hay un médico/
  una farmacia?
I need medecine for …
  Necesito un medicamento
  contra …
How are you?
  ¿Como esta usted?
  (formal, aquaintance)
  ¿Que tal? (friendly)
good – *bien*
My name is …
  Me llamo …
flight departure – *salida*
flight arrival – *llegada*
What time is it?
  ¿Que hora es?
yesterday/today/tomorrow
  ayer/hoy/mañana
How far …?
  ¿Qué distancia …?

Opening hours

The usual business hours are 9.00–13.00 and 16.00–20.00 hrs on workdays, and 9.00–13.00 hrs on Saturdays. There are a number of shops in the tourist centres that are also open on Saturday afternoons and Sundays. Some petrol stations are closed on Sundays and public holidays.

Police

The Guardia Civil is the country and criminal police. They are responsible for fighting crime, but they sometimes deal with traffic police matters. Green uniform, black patent helmet. Tel. 062.

The Policía Municipal, the town police, is in charge of traffic and local matters. Every political community has its *Policía Municipal*, mostly in blue uniform. Tel. 092.

The Policía Nacional is national and is under the control of the Spanish Ministry for the Interior. They are responsible for residence and work permits, as well as "lost" notices. The uniform is khaki with a dark brown beret. Tel. 091.

Post

The main post office and telegramme office is in Arrecife: Correos y Telégrafos. Avenida General Franco, no. 8. Tel. 928 80 06 73. Open Monday–Saturday 9.00–14.00 hrs. Telegrams can be collected until 20.30. Post office is *correo*, letter *carta*, post card *postal*, stamp *sello*. You can find out the various postal charges by looking them up on the list hanging in the post office. You can also have your mail franked and sent out by the hotel reception.

Press

Foreign newspapers and magazines arrive on the island one or two days after publication and cost a lot more than at home.

Provinces

The Canary Islands make up two of Spain's 52 provinces: the Santa Cruz de Tenerife province, covering the islands Tenerife, La Palma, La Gomera and El Hierro, and the Las Palmas de Grand Canaria province, covering Gran Canaria, Fuerteventura and Lanzarote.

Public holidays

Maundy Thursday *(Jueves Santo)*, Good Friday *(Viernes Santo)* and Corpus Christi *(Día del Corpus)* are movable holidays. In addition there are the village festivals or *fiestas*. For the main dates of these, refer to the descriptions of the individual towns and villages.

1st January
New Year *(Año Nuevo)*
6th January
Epiphany *(Los Reyes)*
2nd February
Candlemas (Purification of the

Virgin Mary) *(La Candelaria)*
19 March
St Joseph's Day *(San José)*
1st May
International Labour Day
(Día de Trabajo)
30th May
Canary's Day *(Día de Canarias)*
29th June
Peter and Paul *(Pedro y Paulo)*
25th July
St John the Baptist's Day
(Santiago Apóstol)
15th August
Ascension Day *(Asunción)*
12th October
Discovery of America *(Día de la Hispanidad)*
1st November
All Saints' Day
(Todos los Santos)
8th December
Immaculate Conception of the Virgin Mary *(Immaculada Concepción)*
24th December
Christmas Eve *(La Nochebuena)*
25th December
Christmas Day *(Navidad)*

Reserva de la Biosfera

In 1976, UNESCO began declaring regions all over the world biosphere reservations, which are given particular protection and conservation measures. At the end of 1993 UNESCO declared Lanzarote a biosphere reservation. This is not least due to César Manrique's efforts to create gentle, nature-oriented and environmentally aware tourism. More and more of Lanzarote's inhabitants are joining in, with growing environmental awareness and environmentally friendly behaviour. Please do your bit to save the environment!

Settling in

Acclimatisation between two to three days. You should not expose yourself much to sun and sea in these days. Changing from a cool temperate, European climate to a subtropical one is often more difficult than one thinks.

Shopping

Since 1852 the Canary Islands have been a free trade zone, Tobacco, spirits and perfume are considerably cheaper than in Europe. Not every trader passes on the tax concessions to the customer, especially in the case of photographic or electrical goods. These goods should be tested very thoroughly. Bargaining is usual in Indian and Moroccan bazaars.

Souvenirs

Handfinished embroidery, called *calados*, which are made into the form of table cloths, sets, rugs and blouses, are among the more authentic souvenirs (beware of imitations). Patterned embroidery, *bordados*, come from La Palma along with black ceramics and basketware. Good quality ceramics can be found on all the islands. The

Canary knives, which Canary farmers carry when working on the fields, are just as authentic. The knives are used at lunch or snack times and have decorative handles. On Lanzarote you can buy a *timple*, or Francigi miniatures. Along with stationery such as maps, calendars, brochures and books, natural produce is also a popular souvenir. For instance there are the delicious wines from El Hierro and Lanzarote or the banana liquer, a Canary speciality, handfinished cigars and bunches of strelitzia. Since the Canary Islands are a duty free zone, luxury goods are much cheaper. You should test both the good and the price, since the concession is often not passed onto the customer or the good is of poor quality.

Sport

Lanzarote is a paradise for sport lovers. Almost all the larger hotels and some apartment complexes have their own sports facilities. There are tennis courts, some floodlit, squash courts, volleyball fields and bowling alleys. You can hire bicycles and fly a kite, ride, climb, and play golf or darts, and there is also archery. But the most popular sports are of course water sports:

Deep-sea angling: You can go out on deep-sea angling trips to catch tuna, bonitos, barracuda, sharks, marlin and wahoo. The most prized catch is a swordfish. Please inquire at your own reception.

Sailing: If you want to hire a sailing boat, inquire at Catlanza in Puerto Calero. Tel. 928 51 30 22. Fax 928 51 10 01.

Wind-surfing: The Canary Isles waters are well-known as good wind-surfing. There are wind-surfing schools at the Playa de las Cucharas on the Costa Teguise, at the Playa de Matagorda in Puerto del Carmen, and at the Playa Blanca. The La Santa sports facility, which has a lake, is ideal for learners.

Diving: There are diving bases in Costa Teguise, Arrieta, La Santa, Puerto del Carmen, Puerto Calero, Playa Quemada and Playa Blanca. These are kept by diving schools. If you want to go in for independent diving, you should first inquire about currents. Underwater hunting is not permitted along all stretches of the coast, compressed-air harpoons are completely prohibited. Give the physallia carabella (a kind of jellyfish), which comes sometimes close to the cost during the summer, a wide berth. Its stings, 6−7 cm in length, are caustic to the touch, and can cause paralysis. The islanders treat the burns with garlic and onion juice. You should also beware of the moray, whose blood and bites are venomous. There are no dangerous sharks close to the coast. The thornback ray has a span of up to 2.5 m and is fascinating to watch.

Surfing: There are good conditions for surfing on the north coast of Lanzarote, at the Playa de Famara by La Santa and at the Playa de la Cantería by Orzola. On the east coast, only the coastline between Punta de Mujeres and Los Jameos del Agua is worth mentioning.

The ECONATURA group offers a wide range of adventure, sports, and leisure activities, supervised by well-trained young people. The focus is on active tourism that respects the environment. You can take part in the following activities: walking, kayaking, archery, fishing, mountain-biking, climbing, riding and others. ECONATURA, on the main road between Mala and Arrieta. Tel. 928 17 31 06.

Canary Island sports:

The Canary Islanders love football and Vela Latina. A form of pole-vault known as *salto del regatón* has developed on La Palma. *Lucha canaria*, or Canary Island wrestling, is widespread on all the islands except Gomera.

Lucha canaria:

The *lucha canaria* is reminiscent of Celtic wrestling, but this particular type is known only on the Canary Islands. According to some sources, the sport was practised in Egypt. At the very least, there are some parallels in the reliefs of Beni Hassan, which depict situations in a wrestling match. It is a martial art typical of the Ancient Canarians, who liked to test their strength a their festivals – and present-day islanders still do. The *lucha canaria* is held at every *fiesta*, on a ground called the *terrero*. This is a double ring with a floor of hardtrodden earth or sawdust. The inner ring measures 10 metres, the outer ring 11. The wrestlers are called *pollos* (fighting cocks); successfull ones are worshipped like football stars. They wear thin shirts and short trousers of linen, with the legs rolled up. The adversary grips hold of these trousers. The *pollos* fight barefoot. The fight is fair, as the opening ritual proves. Each team consists of eleven fighters. There is a maximum of three rounds, each round lasting three minutes at the most. The winner is the one who throws his opponent twice. This has to be inside the inner ring, or between the inner and outer rings provided the winner remains inside the inner ring. The victor can continue fighting for up to three more fights. Each fighter has to fight every member of the opposing team. The best have a mastery of all the 43 holds that are allowed – beginners have to have a command of five holds.

Stick game: The stick game has also been handed down from the Ancient Canarians. The aim of the stick fighters used to be to defend themselves against attack without killing or seriously injuring their opponents. There are two different types: fencing with flexible rods known as *varas*, and fencing with rough sticks called *palos*. The players' feet are not allowed to move from the spot, so the players can only parry blows or bend their upper bodies to avoid being hit. All in all, fighters are supposed to move their bodies as little as possible during the fights. Only men use the *varas*, while in the *palos* fights, there may be matches between men and women.

Taxi

The main numbers:
Arrecife
Tel. 928 80 31 04
Costa Teguise
Tel. 928 59 08 63, 928 59 00 95, 928 59 01 60
Puerto del Carmen
Tel. 928 51 36 34, 928 51 11 36, 928 51 36 38, 928 51 36 35
Playa Blanca
Tel. 928 51 71 36, 928 51 72 51.

Telephones

The cheapest telephones to use are the ones in post offices or public telephone boxes – in hotels, telephone calls cost twice as much. Public telephones take 5, 25 and 100 Ptas. coins. Local calls cost 5 Ptas. Insert at least three coins at the start of your call. There are detailed instructions in most telephones boxes. First dial 00 (for an international call). When you hear a continu-

ous, high-pitched tone, dial the code for your country.

Austria	43
Denmark	45
Finland	358
Germany	49
Ireland	353
Norway	47
Sweden	46
Switzerland	41
United Kingdom	40

Time

The Canary Islands have Western European Time, which is the same as GMT, so visitors from the U. K. or Ireland for example, will usually not have to change their watches. However, there may be some overlap when clocks are put back for winter time and forward for summer time.

Tips

As a general rule, you should give tips of between 5% and 10%. Hotel and restaurant bills include 15% service charge. You should give your room cleaner at least 500 Ptas. per week. Waiters, bar staff, taxidrivers, travel guides, coach drivers on excursions, ushers, porters and doormen also expect to be tipped.

Tourist information

Arrecife: Parque Municipal, Tel. 928 81 18 60. Open Mon–Fri 8.00–14.00 and 17.00–19.00 hrs, Sat 8.00–12.00 hrs.
Puerto del Carmen: Avenida de

las Playas in the pavilion opposite Calle Anzelo. Tel. 928 51 53 37. Open Mon–Fri 9.00–13.00 hrs.
Playa Blanca: In the harbour building. Tel. 928 51 77 94. Open Mon–Fri 9.00–13.00 hrs.

Turismo Rural

Holidays in the country have really taken off in Lanzarote. If this is the kind of holiday for you, the interior of the island has houses with remarkable architecture where you can stay and still have quality and service. One of the places you can inquire and book is: Viajes La Alegranza, Calle Canalejas, 23 in Arrecife. Tel. 928 80 36 14. Fax 928 80 42 09.

Valuables

Look after your valuables. It is not advisable to leave anything in your car. Some hotels have room safes. It is usually possible to hand valuables in at the reception for safekeeping.

Walking

There is first-class walking country on Lanzarote, with a lot of paths across the plains that are relatively easy to find. Only organized walkers with special permission are allowed to walk through the National Park. You can get information from the Centro de Visitantes. Tel. 928 84 08 39. Even if the mountains on Lanzarote hardly go above 600 metres in height, don't underestimate them. You have to be sure-footed and vertigo-free, and in some places even need mountain experience. Particular caution is advised at the Risco de Famara, a route equivalent to a difficult and dangerous open mountain trek, and you will need climbing experience. And watch out for falling rocks! Always take strong shoes, a head covering, anorak, and clothes covering the entire body. Take plenty of drinking-water and don't forget your sunglasses. Organized walks are available, inquire at your own reception or at: ECO-NATURA on the main road between Mala and Arrieta. Tel./Fax 928 17 31 06.

■

6. INDEX

189

7. FURTHER READING

Abercromby, J.: **A study of the ancient inhabitants of the Canary Islands Man 1**, London 1917 · Alonso, J.: **Preliminary findings of a study in progress on consanguinity in the Canary Islands**, Simp. Antrop. Biol. España, Madrid 1978 · Bannerman, D. A.: **The Canary Islands. Their history, natural history and scenery**, Gurney & Jackson, London 1922 · Bannerman, D. A.: **Birds of the Atlantic Islands**, Vol. 1 (A history of the birds of the Canary Islands and of the Salvages) Oliver & Boyd, Edinburgh/London 1963 · Bramwell, D.: **The endemic flora of the Canary Islands**, KBEC 1976 · Bramwell, D. & Z.: **Wild Flowers of the Canary Islands**, Santa Cruz de Tenerife 1974 · Cook, Alice Carter: **The aborigines of the Canary Islands**, American Anthropologist 1900 · De La Nuez Caballero: **Contemporary Poetry from the Canary Islands**, 10/93 Dufour Editions · Espinosa, Fray Alonso de: **The guanches of Tenerife. The holy image of Our Lady of Candelaria and the Spanish conquest and settlement**, Hakluyt Society, Cambridge 1907 · Fernandez Armesto, Felipe: **The Canary Islands after the conquest. The making of a colonial society in the early sixteenth century**, Oxford Historical Monographs IX Clarendon Press, Oxford 1982 · Fuster; J. M.; et al.: **Geology and vulcanology of the Canary Islands Lanzarote**, Inst. Lucas Mallada, Spec. Publ., Madrid 1968 · Katsui, Y. (Ed.): **List of the world's active volcanoes**, Spec. Issue of the Bull of Volc. Eruptions, Tokio 1971 · Krüss, J. R.: **The names of the Canary Islands and their verification**, KBEC 1976 · Kunkel, G. (Ed.): **Biogeography and Ecology in the Canary Islands** in: Monographiae Biologicae, Vol. 30, The Hague 1976 · López Herrera, Salvador: **The Canary Islands through history**, Ed. Dosbe, Madrid 1978 · Major, R. H.: **The Canarian, or book of the conquest and conversion of the Canarians in the year 1402**, Hakluyt Society, London 1872 · Mason, John & Anne: **The Canary Islands**, Batsford Publ., London 1976 · Mercer, J.: **The Canary Islands. Their prehistory, conquest and survival**, Collings, London 1980 · Nichols, Thomas: **A pleasant description of the fortunate landes**, London 1583 · Schwidetzki, I.: **Population biology of the Canary Islands** MCXL I 1982

LANZAROTE & CÉSAR MANRIQUE 7 MONUMENTS

The book describes Lanazrote's seven major sights designed by César Manrique: Jameos del Agua, Monumento al Campesino, Restaurant el Diablo, Mirador del Río, Castillo San José, Jardín de Cactus and the Fundación César Manrique, 60 pages with 72 photographs, Text: Wolfgang Borsich, Photography: Pedro Velázquez and Wolfgang Borsich.

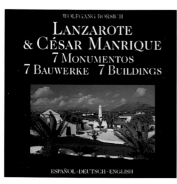

YEAR CALENDAR OF LANZAROTE

Every year we produce a calendar with our most beautiful photographs. Format 33 x 44 cm. With a strong cardboard container and polythene sealed, it travels safely. The ideal present to take back home.

MRS LISA

Mrs Lisa is a picture book for children from age three. It tells the story of a dog that lives by the sea. Text: Wolfgang Borsich. Illustrations: Jan Cerny.

Wolfgang Borsich / Jan Černý
Mrs Lisa

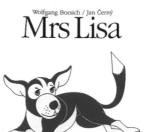

THE MAP OF LANZAROTE

The map of Lanzarote, our road map with a wealth of informative contents and comprehensive cartography, and with a brief guide in words and pictures, describing the major places and sights, with notes on Canary Isles food, recommended restaurants, recommended accommodation and all the information you need.

INFORMATION

TEXT & FIRST DRAFT
WOLFGANG BORSICH

PHOTOGRAPHY
WOLFGANG BORSICH, PETER SICKERT;
JOSÉ MARÍA BARRETO CAAMAÑO
WALTER FOGEL, BARBARA GRAF, JESÚS PORÍEROS VALVERDE
UDO REUSCHLING

PHOTOGRAPHIC EDITORS
WOLFGANG BORSICH, NIEVES GONZÁLEZ HERNÁNDEZ

GRAPHIC CONCEPT & TYPOGRAPHY
PETER SICKERT

LAYOUT
PETER SICKERT, WOLFGANG BORSICH

MAPS & DRAWING
KARTOGRAFIE HUBER, GERD OBERLÄNDER
MUNICH

ILLUSTRATIONS
WE ARE ESPECIALLY GREATEFUL TO THE COLEGIO DE
ARQUITECTOS DE CANARIAS, DEMARCACIÓN DE TENERIFE,
LA GOMERA Y EL HIERRO, ARCHIVO HISTÓRICO,
FOR PERMISSION TO PRINT THE DREAWINGS BY LEONARDO TORRIANI
ON PAGES 8, 9 AND 12.

ISBN
84-930273-0-8

DEPOSITO LEGAL
M-8.682-2000

IMPRIME
Cromoimagen, S.L. Albasanz, 14 Bis • 28037 Madrid